BBC

Springwatch

UNSPRUNG

Why Do Robins Have Red Breasts?

BBC Springwatch UNSPRUNG

Why Do Robins Have Red Breasts?

All Your Wildlife Questions Answered

Joanne Stevens
and the Springwatch Team

Martin Hughes-Games

Collins

First published in 2013 by Collins

An imprint of HarperCollins*Publishers*
77–85 Fulham Palace Road
Hammersmith, London W6 8JB

www.harpercollins.co.uk

10 9 8 7 6 5 4 3 2 1

A catalogue record for this book is
available from the British Library.

ISBN 978-0-00-749817-8

Printed and bound in Great Britain by
Clays Ltd, St Ives plc.

MIX
Paper from
responsible sources
FSC
www.fsc.org   **FSC˚ C007454**

FSC™ is a non-profit international organisation established to promote
the responsible management of the world's forests. Products carrying the
FSC label are independently certified to assure consumers that they come
from forests that are managed to meet the social, economic and
ecological needs of present and future generations,
and other controlled sources.

Find out more about HarperCollins and the environment at
www.harpercollins.co.uk/green

Dedication

For my parents, who always encouraged me to go outside and have little adventures.

Contents

Introduction   1

Spring   5
Summer   65
Autumn   127
Winter   189

Sources of Information and Inspiration   249
Acknowledgements   261
About the Authors   263
Index   265

Introduction

Since *Springwatch* first hit our television screens back in 2005, the series has developed an enduring two-way relationship with its audience that is unique in UK broadcasting. *Springwatch* tapped into the public's passion for natural history and invited the audience to get involved, ask questions and share their experiences of observing their local wildlife. It started with good old-fashioned letters, videotapes and comments on the programme's website, but the conversation has today evolved to various social media networks like Facebook, Flickr and Twitter. Whatever the method of communication, one thing remains the same – the audience's undimmed enthusiasm and endless thirst for knowledge.

By 2009, frankly, the show was inundated; thousands of beautiful photos, hundreds of hours of interesting footage and countless intriguing queries poured in from the audience. To accommodate all of this brilliant content a sister show called *Springwatch Unsprung* was spawned, with the inimitable Martin Hughes-Games at the helm. Subsequently, *Autumnwatch* and *Winterwatch* also gained their own version of *Unsprung*. Like its host, *Unsprung* can be anarchic, chaotic and irreverent, but at its heart lies a desire to rekindle a child-like wonder and curiosity about nature. It includes quizzes, live animal guests, artists and other guests who make a living from or have a hobby that involves nature. As a live, unscripted and unrehearsed show anything can happen – and it often does. Ultimately, though, *Unsprung* is made by the audience; without their input the show simply wouldn't exist.

Still, even with *Unsprung*, there just wasn't enough airtime to answer all the compelling questions that were sent in – proof, if it were needed, that UK wildlife can be just as fascinating as exotic foreign species. Hence this book, as an effort to scratch that metaphorical itch of a nagging wildlife query. You know what it's like ... those niggling but profound questions in life that strike when you're walking to work, pottering in the garden or beachcombing with the kids (children always seem to ask the simplest but most challenging questions!). Why do ladybirds have spots? Do snails get slower with age? How do moths find their way in the dark? Do oysters dream? And why, oh why, do dogs love rolling in fox poo?!

You'll find the answers to all these and other equally perplexing questions in this book, arranged by season. Martin Hughes-Games has written an introduction to each section to inspire, inform and boost your natural history knowledge so that you can impress (?!) your friends in the pub. There are some mind-boggling quizzes thrown in for good measure too. And if reading about nature spurs you into action in the real world, there's a selection of wildlife organisations that would welcome your support and involvement. While *Unsprung* can't be re-created exactly on paper, hopefully its spirit shines through in these pages.

Spring

Spring – surely our most uplifting and optimistic season? The thrill of seeing the first flowers, usually the lesser celandine with its gleaming golden petals, the naughty green shoots of Arum (lords and ladies) poking through the brown debris of winter (a plant which probably has more rude colloquial names than any other UK plant, due to the shape of its phallic stamen within the fold of the first leaf), and the shattering sight and smell of a bluebell wood, seemingly hovering an inch or two above reality. How can it be so dazzling? The colours are almost unreal, created from nothing more than air, sunlight and water, with a pinch of minerals from the soil. Magic.

Along with the bluebells there are often great swathes of powerful-smelling ramsons at this time of year. A girlfriend once cooked me a quiche flavoured with ramsons (wild garlic). It was, honesty compelled me to be frank, quite horrid and I foolishly said as much. That was some 30 years ago and she's still not forgiven me!

Suddenly eggs appear in nest boxes as my chickens start to lay again after a winter of rest. Soon I'm making holes in compost with a pencil to plant tomato seeds. Then there's the almost forgotten sensation of the Sun's warmth on bare skin pring is one of the glories of living in the UK because, se, in some countries the different seasons are not so defined – they cannot enjoy this incredible sense of rebirth after a gloomy, desolate winter as new life explodes all across the countryside.

In early April I scan the sky with a mounting sense of expectation. Then, suddenly, there it is – the first swallow of the year, sweeping through the sky, chesting up on the breeze, all the way from Africa, bringing with it the promise of warm days to come.

There are a host of things to see and do in spring. Watch out for migrating toads early in the year; thousands of them wake up from their winter torpor and start to march, en masse, towards their favourite breeding ponds. This can be a seriously impressive spectacle. Writing in 1188, Gerald of Wales slightly misinterpreted the toad migration:

> 'In our own days,' he says, 'a young man was persecuted by a plague of toads. It seemed as if the entire population of toads had made an agreement to visit him. Toads came flocking from all directions, more and more of them until no one could count them. In the end the young man's friends who were trying to help were quite worn out.'

So far so good, but then Gerald comes off the rails – as ever, scientific verisimilitude thrown out the window for the sake of a good yarn:

'The toads killed him and ate him right up leaving nothing but his skeleton!'

Migrating toads often have to cross roads and passing cars can, inadvertently, cause carnage. If you would like to help you can find local toad patrols at www.froglife.org/toadsonroads.

I'm going to feature a special 'Unsprung' word for each season, and the one for spring is 'guffing'. Male newts display to the females underwater and at the end of their display they sometimes come up close and blow a bubble of air at her as if to say, 'I did all that and still have air to spare!' This bubble blowing is called 'guffing'.

Chris Packham and I went badger watching recently and it's surprisingly exciting – as Chris says, you keep thinking something is going to emerge from the sett entrance in the next 30 seconds. Badger watching is especially rewarding in spring as the youngsters make their first appearance above ground and, having been stuck underground in the sett for many weeks, they tend to be particularly feisty. There are many local badger watching groups to be found at www.badger.org.uk/content/Living.asp.

Of course, spring wouldn't be spring without mad March hares. I was once filming for *Springwatch* on Isla with Simon King and he suddenly said 'quick, quick! Those hares over there – start filming them!'. Frankly I was bemused, it was interesting to see hares, there were six of them all together, but ...? Gradually Simon, as only Simon can, revealed the real drama of what was going on. There was one female, just coming into season, and the other five hares were potential suitors. It was fascinating to watch the males chasing the female in turn and seeing her beat them off (and the fur really flies) until, finally, she made her choice. Fighting 'mad March hares' are generally females beating off unwelcome suitors, not males fighting each other.

The dawn chorus is one of the greatest wildlife experiences it is possible to have – no, honestly! – and it peaks in spring. Why not get up at first light, make a nourishing cup of tea and step outside into a magical world, a symphony of natural sound. I guarantee you'll feel uplifted for the rest of the day. If you want to find out who's making all the music there are organised dawn chorus walks up and down the country, look up your nearest one on: www.countryfile.com/countryside/top-10-dawn-chorus-walks.

The date I hear the drone of my first bumblebee of the year goes straight into the diary. It's another joyful reminder that summer is on its way. In fact, we have no less than 25 different species of bumblebee. The first ones you see and hear will all be queens who, having hibernated all winter, are now prospecting to find a place in which to nest and start a new colony, often an old mouse hole. If it's a cold morning and you hear a subdued buzzing sound coming from one place, have a look and you might see something curious. Bees have to 'warm up' flight muscles to a critical temperature (30°C) before they can actually take off. To do this they disengage their wings, then activate the muscles which warm up, without the wings moving (rather like pushing down the clutch in the car and revving the engine), then, once the critical temperature is reached, the wings are re-engaged and the bee takes off. Magic! There's a lovely video of this on the BBC website: www.bbc.co.uk/nature/life/Bumblebee#intro.

Moths and other flying insects do this too.

To help bees, moths and butterflies in your garden why not plant flowers specifically to provide food and shelter for them? Best of all, plant a sequence of plants that will flower all year. There's some useful advice on the best way to do this at: www.butterfly-conservation.org/93/give-time.html.

Finally, if you are really serious about helping wildlife, get in touch with your local rescue centre. This time of year they are often inundated with injured and abandoned baby animals, fox and badger cubs, deer and a host of birds. They often welcome volunteers and you will find yourself intimately involved in helping to care for wildlife. It's an emotional roller coaster, though, once you get involved, so be warned!

At a Snail's Pace

How long do snails live? Do they get slower with age?
Nature Lover

Both the lifespan and speed of a snail vary according to the
species. There are thousands of snail species worldwide but
of those only about twenty are regularly found in our
gardens. Whether or not they live to a ripe old age depends
on how well they avoid parasites, disease or predators – and
there are plenty of these around; thrushes in particular will
readily make a meal of a juicy snail or two. Most snails will
survive for only two or three years, but Edible or Roman
snails (*Helix pomatia*) can live for several decades – the oldest
known individual reached an impressive 35 years old.

As well as predators and parasites, snails also have to
endure extreme weather conditions. They have adapted to
survive several months of dry or cold weather by covering
their shell opening with an epiphragm – a layer of mucus
that dries out to form a barrier which prevents water loss.
Some species, such as the Roman snail, can produce a much
more substantial and solid epiphragm which is reinforced
with calcium carbonate before the mollusc goes into
hibernation. Snails can also protect themselves in winter by
changing the composition of their blood, or haemolymph, to
prevent it freezing. The common garden snail (*Helix aspersa*)
can survive in temperatures down to minus 5 degrees
Celsius.

Snails are renowned for their slowness, but they have no need to rush anywhere. The majority of species are herbivores, so they don't have to chase after prey, and to escape most predators they need only to retreat within their shell. Snails may be slow but they are strong; when tested, one species was able to drag 50 times its own weight horizontally and nine times its weight vertically.

A snail moves by expanding and contracting its muscular foot in waves, and as it does so it secretes a slimy mucus that lubricates its path and reduces any friction on the surface beneath. You can watch how they do this by putting one on a clean drinking glass or windowpane. If you liquidise a little lettuce and smear some on the glass you may be able to see their tongue, or radula, in action too. While you're there, you could test their speed. Garden snails can crawl up to 1.3 centimetres per second, equivalent to about 0.05 km/h. The fastest known garden snail was called Archie. 'He' (snails are hermaphrodites) slithered 33 centimetres in two minutes at the 1995 World Snail Racing Championships held in Norfolk. At the time of writing, Archie's world record remains unbroken.

Archie's racing days were numbered, though, because like most of us, he would have got slower with age. Scientists often use the common pond snail, *Lymnaea stagnalis*, as a model species for studying the central nervous system and investigating how brains change with age. Results so far show that older pond snails are more forgetful than young ones and feed more slowly. It seems that geriatric snails are generally more sluggish ...

Flying the Nest

What happens to fledglings during their first few nights in the big world? Do the parents stay close by or do they call throughout the night as reassurance to the young? Or, apart from feeding, are the young basically alone?
Tony from Gloucester

When fledglings leave the nest, am I right in assuming they never return to it? In which case, where do they spend their first night outdoors? I know that the nests get quite dirty and parasite-ridden, but even so it seems awfully harsh that they spend all their young lives in the safety of a warm nest and then – BAM! – just like that they're out on their own, never to return? *Kate*

How 'capable' should blue tits be when they fledge? I have a blue tit nest in the vent of an extractor fan and the three young left the nest two days ago. They were feathery but barely able to toddle, let alone fly, and showed no inclination at all to seek shelter or move away from a potential predator – me. Five hours later, when almost fully dark, two were still sitting out in the open on my doorstep cheeping loudly. I haven't seen them since, dead or alive, but they didn't look like survivors. Did they jump too soon, or are blue tit babies always like this?
Stocksfield

Leaving the nest is one of the most dangerous times in a bird's life. Fledglings need to learn fast; they have to work out how to fly, find their own food and avoid becoming someone else's dinner. Mortality is high and many blue tit chicks don't make it – only 38 per cent live for over a year. This is why blue tits lay so many eggs in a clutch (usually 8–10 but up to 16), to increase the chances of at least some of them living to adulthood.

Once chicks of garden birds leave the nest, they rarely return. As Kate points out, the nest is pretty smelly after having a growing family squeezed into it for a while, with droppings and food remains building up. That scent can attract predators. Instead, it is safer for chicks to leave the nest and venture out into the big wide world.

Many garden birds fledge just before they can fly and blackbird chicks leave the nest two or three days before they can take to the air. Fledglings often split up and hide in inconspicuous places, waiting to be fed by their parents. From the parents' point of view, it's safer to split up their offspring around a garden than risk keeping them together where, if found, all the chicks may be taken. Blue tit parents encourage their chicks to leave the nest by enticing them with food and calling to them. Those blue tits chirping on the doorstep were certainly in a risky position, as usually parents would guide their youngsters to a safe place.

If you do find an apparently abandoned chick, don't be tempted to 'save' it too hastily. Instead, try leaving it alone and watch from a distance unless it is in immediate danger or very exposed, in which case move it quickly and gently into some cover, like a bush. The parents are probably nearby and will return to look after it when the coast is clear. Fledgling blue tits usually stay with their parents for a couple of weeks, relying on them for food initially while they learn how to be a blue tit and fend for themselves.

Angry Birds

Why do blue tits fly up to windows and try to 'attack' their reflections? *Cal*

During the breeding season, birds are fired up by hormones and males can become particularly feisty, especially if they are trying to defend a territory. If the resident male catches sight of his reflection in a window, car wing mirror or other shiny surface he will try to see off the apparent 'intruder'. It is most common to see this behaviour in spring, but birds that hold territories throughout the year, such as robins and grey wagtails, may be up for a fight at almost any time. A robin wouldn't hang around attacking a mirror for long, though, as it defends its patch by finding a higher perch than its rival and would soon lose its reflection. An angry bird can be very persistent, keeping up the aggression for hours or sometimes days – this intruder just won't leave! Usually the bird won't hurt itself but it is a huge waste of their time and energy. If you're concerned (or irritated!) you can help to remove the reflection by covering the window or mirror with paper or fabric.

You may be wondering why the bird doesn't recognise its own reflection like we would. Natural reflections are rare and would soon disappear if attacked, for example in a puddle or pond. Very few animal species have been shown to recognise their own reflection, but biologists are very interested in this ability because it can give an insight into how animals' minds work. To find out if an animal can recognise itself in a mirror, biologists put a coloured mark somewhere on its body while it's unconscious or asleep in a place that it would only be able to see in a mirror, for example under its chin or on the end of its nose. If the animal pays attention to the mark in its reflection and touches its skin then this suggests that the animal understands that the reflection is itself. The ability to recognise oneself in a mirror suggests some kind of self-awareness.

A human baby doesn't work out that the infant it can see in the mirror is actually itself until it reaches about 18 months old. This is about the same time that children develop what's called a 'theory of mind'; that is, they can infer what other people are thinking or feeling and begin to be able to put themselves in someone else's shoes. Whether animals can do the same is a matter of huge debate among biologists who study animal behaviour. So far the only other animals shown to recognise their own reflections are similarly large-brained mammals such as chimpanzees, orangutans, elephants and bottlenose dolphins. However, there is one bird that has passed the mirror test: the magpie. Members of the crow family have been shown to be very intelligent, but does this mean that they are self-aware too …? It's certainly food for thought.

No Place Like Home

Limpets – do they return to exactly the same place each time the tide goes out? I've noticed the ones stuck to irregular surfaces have the fringe of their shell shaped to fit the surface (like a jigsaw puzzle), so they must return to the same spot and shuffle around to exactly the same orientation too. Who'd have thought that? Incredible! Or am I wrong? *Steve, Edinburgh*

Steve is absolutely right. Limpets are true homebodies, returning to exactly the same spot on the rocky shore at each tide. As they settle into position, their shells grind against the rock and, over time, they form an indentation called a scar. The limpet's shell fits snugly against this scar and forms a tight seal that prevents the limpets drying out when the tide goes out. Like many animals that live on the shore, they have to tolerate the cycle of being exposed and inundated by seawater twice a day. They also have to endure strong wave action, drying out (limpets can survive up to 65 per cent water loss) and alternating extremes of temperature – from baking in the summer sun (well, sometimes!) to freezing cold seawater. Limpets are tough!

They're also renowned for their ability to cling onto the rock using their powerful, muscular foot for suction and 'glue' for adhesion. This not only helps them to retain water but also deters predators such as birds. That's not their only defence, though; limpets use moves that a wrestler would be proud of! They can 'mushroom', lifting their shell upwards then bringing it down suddenly, stomping on any starfish or other marine predator that comes too close.

At only six centimetres across and three centimetres high it's easy to underestimate these apparently simple creatures, but limpets are architects of their environment. Their grazing keeps algal growth in check, removing young seaweeds. They have a special rasping organ called a radula with sharp 'teeth' set in 160 rows, each containing 12 teeth. Their tips are hardened with iron and silica. Limpets move across the rocks, grazing on a thin film of algae or small larvae. You may be able to see the scraping marks, pale zigzag lines, left behind on the rocks. As they slowly wander across the rocks they leave a trail of mucus in their wake. Before the waters recede, each limpet retraces its route, following chemical cues in the mucus, back to its home scar. The mucus also increases the amount of algae that settles and grows, so in effect the limpets are 'farming' their food. There's much more to the humble limpet than meets the eye.

Oyster Beds

How do shoreline creatures ever sleep? And do oysters and other such shellfish dream? *Tedbun*

This is a deceptively simple question that's actually fiendishly difficult to answer. That's because sleep is something of a biological enigma and biologists grapple even to agree on a definition of what constitutes sleep or why it's necessary. If you think about it, it makes no sense for an animal to stop paying attention to the world around it when there are so many potential dangers. So there must be a really good biological reason for it beyond simply resting – we just haven't worked out what that is yet!

All animals go through periods of activity and inactivity, even those that live on a shoreline and are bashed about by waves. Physiologically, sleeping animals usually have certain brainwave patterns, appear unconscious and have relaxed muscles (except some birds and marine mammals that would fall out of the sky or drown if they relaxed – see the later question about swifts sleeping on the wing, page 82). It's fairly easy to recognise when mammals and birds are asleep, but what about animals such as oysters and shellfish? Many researchers have relied on assessing the brain activity of animals to determine if they are asleep or not, but what happens if an animal has only a simple nervous system and no brain? How can you tell if an invertebrate, such as a fruit fly, is asleep or just stationary? Well, biologists have devised experiments to investigate exactly that. We're all familiar with the fuggy-headedness that comes with a lack of sleep – our cognitive abilities such as learning become impaired, and the same is true for other animals. When deprived of sleep, fruit flies take longer to learn and become more forgetful. And, just like us, some invertebrates that are denied sleep will try to catch up by sleeping longer at the next opportunity. Studies on honeybees, cockroaches, cuttlefish and crayfish suggest that they all experience a kind of sleep, and some biologists suspect that a sleep-like status is universal to all animals.

What about dreaming? In humans, dreams usually occur during one stage of sleep called REM (rapid eye movement) sleep, a state with particular brain activity that most mammals and some birds also experience. It's difficult to prove but some higher mammals do appear to dream – just ask any dog owner who has watched their sleeping hound twitch and whimper after some imaginary squirrel or bone! However, there's no concrete proof of fish, reptiles or any invertebrates falling into REM sleep. So oysters and other shellfish may be lulled to sleep by the sound of the ocean but they probably don't dream.

Shenanigans in the Shrubbery

Can you explain a strange behaviour we've recently witnessed? Dunnocks live in our pyracantha hedge by our back door and feed and drink below it. One dunnock, presumably female, stands still and presents its rear end – tail erect and feathers well fluffed up – and allows its partner to gently peck its bottom repeatedly. This happens time and time again. Is this birdie foreplay? *Mr and Mrs H*

Behind the dull grey and brown plumage of the dunnock (also known as a hedge sparrow, though it's not a sparrow at all) lies a story of sexual intrigue and behaviour worthy of any soap opera. Their name means 'little brown one' but this shy, reclusive bird has a rather colourful and promiscuous lifestyle.

In most species of birds, monogamy is the norm – at least on the surface, though quite a few will skulk off for what are quaintly called 'extra-pair copulations'. Dunnocks, however, have evolved a system where infidelity is par for the course. They use various mating strategies, including love triangles and secret affairs as well as good, old-fashioned monogamy.

Some females breed with two (or more) males, which is a relationship known as polyandry. She mates with both simultaneously, often producing a brood with mixed paternity. By being promiscuous, the female is maximising the chances of her chicks surviving because both fathers will bring food to the nest. Each father will adjust his feeding rate according to how exclusive his relationship was with the mother – the more matings he had, the more likely he is to be the father and the more food he will provide for the nestlings.

Some males will mate with several females (polygyny) and there are even more complicated arrangements among several males and females (polygynandry). A male does best by mating with several females while a female is better off with several male partners. Clearly, this may lead to a battle of the sexes, with males and females competing for the greatest reproductive success.

The specific relationships that occur in each area appear to be determined by several factors. Firstly, the sex ratio in the population may be skewed after a harsh winter to have more males than females – males outcompete females for food so the females are less likely to survive. Secondly, areas with dense bushes allow the females to sneak off for 'a bit on the side' more easily. Lastly, each male and female defends its own territory, and if food is scarce the territories need to be larger. The bigger the females' territories are, the harder it is for a male to monopolise mating rights to more than one female. Where food is plentiful, females' territories are more compact and a male has a better chance of patrolling them and successfully seeing off any rivals.

These sneaky sexual shenanigans lead to some interesting courtship behaviour. In a sense, what the Hanhams witnessed was foreplay. By presenting her rear end and twirling her tail coquettishly the female is inviting the male to mate with her. The male, however, wants to ensure his paternity so he pecks at the female's cloaca (her genital opening) to make her eject any sperm from previous matings. He may continue pecking at her for several minutes until he's satisfied that she has got rid of any other male's sperm and he can be sure that it will be his genes making it through to the next generation. The male may spend a huge amount of time trying to guard his female and protect his paternity rights by preventing her mating with other males. Despite his best efforts, the female will regularly escape as soon as his back is turned and solicit matings from his rivals. Mating activity can become quite frenzied, the avian equivalent of a Benny Hill sketch. Males may mate up to 100 times a day, but blink and you'll miss it – the action is all over in just a tenth of a second.

Tough Love

While I was walking my dog round the pond near my house the other day, I noticed a moorhen with three chicks on the water. As I watched them the adult moorhen began to peck the chicks and make them go under the water. I was just wondering if it was teaching them to dive or if it was trying to kill them? *Charlotte*

Moorhens are notoriously violent parents, often 'tousling' their chicks, pecking at them or holding them underwater. It can look quite brutal and it's probably not a pleasant experience for the chick! Why would a parent be so aggressive towards its own offspring? It seems to be a case of tough love to deal with sibling rivalry.

Moorhens often have large broods of eight or more eggs. They hatch over several days so the ones that hatch first are larger and have an advantage in securing their parents' care over the smaller ones. Moorhens are 'nidifugous'; that is, they leave the nest soon after hatching but the chicks are still partly reliant on their parents for food. Most waterfowl, such as mallards, will simply lead their chicks to food and let them get on with it, but moorhens take great care in feeding their young. However, there is intense competition between the chicks for their parents' attention and the adults are constantly pestered for food.

Adults are more aggressive towards larger chicks that may outcompete their smaller siblings and monopolise feeds. Unsurprisingly, after being attacked a chick stays out of its parents' way and stops begging to be fed for a while. This allows the smaller chicks a chance to receive their fair share of food. So the parent may be trying to ensure all chicks are fed equally and also force the bigger chicks to fend for themselves, encouraging them to become independent.

Despite the squabbles, moorhens have very attentive families. Moorhens and long-tailed tits are the only British birds to breed cooperatively; that is, youngsters from the first brood sometimes stick around to help raise the second brood. This gives the juveniles valuable experience in bringing up chicks and helps their siblings to survive. As is so often the case in human families, the older moorhen brothers and sisters support their frazzled parents to keep the peace.

Family Affair

Do fox families contain youngsters from different years in the same den? If so, do the older cubs play any part in rearing their younger siblings? *Alan*

Foxes are usually seen alone but they don't lead solitary lives. Most fox families consist of an adult male and female plus their cubs. When the cubs are born they are just 10–14 centimetres long, blind and helpless. They're completely dependent on their mother for milk and warmth as they cannot regulate their own temperature. She will stay with them around the clock for the first couple of weeks. During this time, the male will bring her food but sometimes the family will be assisted by other adult helpers too, usually vixens. These helpers often don't breed, and when the mother returns to hunting duties they will also help to look after the cubs – groom them, play with them and bring food to the den.

These helpers are often daughters from previous years, but they could also be the main vixen's sisters or even her mother once she has passed breeding age. About one in three fox families has one or more non-breeding vixen helping out, and there's usually a hierarchy so that only the alpha female gives birth. Studies have shown that helpers don't necessarily increase the cubs' chances of survival but they do take the pressure off the parents, which don't have to work so hard to feed the cubs.

So what's in it for the helpers, when they could be raising cubs of their own? It may be a case of 'kin selection', a strategy that means sometimes it's better to help raise a relative's young even at a cost to the individual. When the time comes for a fully-grown cub to disperse, it has to weigh up the costs and benefits of staying against the risks of leaving home. If it stays, the cub may not breed for a year or two but it might inherit the territory. By leaving home the cub may have young of its own by next spring but it must find its own territory first. Mortality can be high for dispersing cubs so it is a difficult choice for them to make.

Choosing to stay at home doesn't always mean that a fox won't get the chance to breed, though. In 2012, *Springwatch* followed a fox family that had a mammoth litter of eleven cubs living under a garden shed in Potter's Bar. Most litters only have four to six cubs so this was unusual. After watching the family closely for several weeks it became apparent that there were actually two adult females, one dominant and one subordinate, and both appeared to suckle the young. It seems that both vixens were mothers and they had pooled their litters to raise them cooperatively.

Dogged by a Bad Smell

Just a quickie, why do dogs love to roll around in fox poo? What is the attraction? *Jackie*

Members of the canine family, such as wolves, dogs and foxes, have a very acute sense of smell. Humans are primarily visual creatures while a canine's world is ruled by scent. Dogs and their wild relatives can pick out the faintest scents using their wet noses and millions of olfactory receptors. A large proportion of a dog's brain is devoted to processing all this olfactory information and their sense of smell may be several million times more sensitive than ours. In the wild they would use this skill to track down prey or other members of their species, but we humans have exploited the dog's nose for a wide variety of tasks, from finding truffles and recovering shot game birds to detecting explosives, illegal drugs and missing people.

Scent is vital in fox communication too. Foxes often mark their territory by defecating in conspicuous places, such as on top of molehills, at the junction of paths or on tussocks of grass. It's thought that a fox's faeces provides clues to the animal's sex, fertility, health and status. Both fox urine and faeces have a distinctive, musky smell that even our weak human noses can easily detect!

Why then, if dogs have such a sensitive nose, would they choose to roll in something as stinky as fox poo? It's thought to be a relic of their wolf ancestors and may have several purposes. Wolves roll in something pungent like a rotting carcass or another species' droppings as a form of olfactory camouflage. They first rub their cheek against the object then slide against it, covering themselves in a foreign scent. This may disguise the wolf's own smell so that it isn't detected by prey when attempting to hunt. Scent rolling may also enable a wolf to bring back any novel scent it finds and share it with the rest of the pack. When the wolf returns it is sniffed and licked by other wolves that then pick up the scent. Another theory is that certain scents may act like perfume or aftershave and make the wolf more attractive to others.

Regardless of the motive, dogs that have rolled in fox poo certainly aren't more attractive to humans! Not only is the smell offensive, it's also unhygienic. Fox droppings may carry diseases and parasites like tapeworms and roundworms, so it goes without saying that if you wash the fox poo off your dog make sure you wash your hands very thoroughly afterwards.

The Sweet Smell of Success

Do starlings like scented nests? Earlier this spring I saw a couple of starlings pulling bits out of my lavender bush and flying off with them, at about the time that they were nesting. I can only assume they like the smell. By the way, I now have approximately 50 starlings – adults and young – feeding in my small town garden. *Sue*

Male starlings have been known to adorn their nest with yarrow, parsley and hawthorn as well as lavender. They might be attempting to court a female by saying it with flowers but it seems that scent is more important than beauty. Several species of birds appear to have a penchant for aromatherapy, not just starlings, and they continue to bring scented plants to the nest once their chicks have hatched.

On *Springwatch*, cameras inside a blue tit nest showed the adults bringing in mint – they didn't feed it to the chicks but placed it around the nest. At first, biologists thought birds might be using aromatic plants to deter parasites such as lice, maggots and ticks, much like we use mothballs. In fact, French biologists have discovered that plants such as mint, lavender and the curry plant are used for their antibacterial properties. Blue tit chicks raised in nests lined with these aromatic plants have fewer bacteria on their skin. This may allow them to put effort into their growth rather than strengthening their immune system. Chicks surrounded by scented leaves appear to grow more quickly and thus have a better chance of survival. Individual blue tits have particular preferences for which plant they collect – some prefer mint while others always collect lavender, even when both herbs are available.

A similar study on starlings showed that the air inside nests lined with fresh herbs is full of volatile compounds – smelly chemicals from the plants' essential oils. They include limonene (citrus-like), myrcene (from thyme) and phellandrene (peppery-minty, like eucalyptus). The aromatic plants were shown to repel mosquitoes as well as inhibit the growth of bacteria; this is advantageous because blood-sucking insects aren't just an annoyance, they can spread diseases to the chicks.

City birds have adapted to their surroundings by using cigarette butts instead of plants to scent their nests. Research in Mexico showed that by lining their nests with the nicotine-infused filters from smoked cigarettes, house sparrows and finches reduced the number of mites and other parasites. Nicotine is a natural insect repellent produced by the tobacco plant as a defence against herbivores, so it's not a surprise that it deters parasites too. Over the years, *Springwatch* has received many photos of blue tits and other birds nesting in cigarette butt bins, so it seems that British birds have learned the same trick.

Hungry Herons

We recently saw a heron catch a wounded bird. It decapitated it then took it to the water's edge and ate it. I thought they were fish eaters, or will they eat other things if it's an easy catch? *Lesley*

How common is it for herons to 'nick' moorhen chicks? This weekend I saw a heron bully two adult moorhens until they moved from the nest and it then nicked a chick and flew off! *Tessie B*

Herons aren't fussy eaters and have a very varied diet which includes small mammals, insects, little birds and amphibians as well as fish. They will catch birds up to the size of a water rail, so moorhen chicks are just a small snack.

Despite their long neck, herons have the same number of vertebrae as other birds but the bones are specially configured so that herons can bend their neck into an 'S' shape, allowing them to strike quickly. Usually, herons rely on stealth for hunting, waiting motionless before launching their long, sharp beak to snatch a fish or other prey. This technique is imaginatively known as 'standing still'. Another technique is 'walking slowly', during which, yes, you've guessed it, they walk at a very slow pace to prevent spooking their prey. However, herons are large birds, standing about a metre high with a two-metre wingspan, so they're not afraid to use brute force and bullying to get a meal if necessary, especially when they have hungry chicks to feed.

The type of food a heron chooses depends on the time of year and what is locally abundant in that season. Pellets collected from breeding colonies provide clues to which prey the adults are catching. Heron chicks are reliant on their parents for a long time, spending about 50 days in the nest, and they may not be independent until they are 80 days old. Herons are very adaptable hunters and can react to changes in prey availability, so the food brought to the chicks may change over the weeks. When there are plenty of small ducklings in May and early June, these can make up a large part of their diet. Some colonies feed mostly on small mammals such as water voles, mice, rats and even young rabbits. Although they are usually seen hunting in or near ponds and rivers, during the winter herons may hunt away from water, looking for small mammals in fields and pastures.

Herons will also make the most of a well-stocked garden pond if they find one, so if you want to hang on to your fish, try covering the pond with a fine mesh net and provide hiding places for the fish by planting waterlilies and other aquatic plants. You can also make it more difficult for herons to get to the water's edge by encircling the pond with a barrier of taut strings or wires 20 centimetres and 35 centimetres above the water level. Herons are pretty bright birds so plastic decoy herons don't appear to be much of a deterrent and may even attract a heron to hunt.

Purrfect

Do wildcats sound the same as domestic cats? Do they purr? *Avril*

As most cat owners know, domestic cats communicate with a variety of calls and vocalisations including hisses, growls, chatters, as well as the more familiar purring and meowing. Hissing and growling are clear signs that a cat is feeling threatened or angry. A female will 'caterwaul' when she is fertile – a bloodcurdling wail that advertises to local males that she is ready to mate. Kittens meow to their mothers to request food or attention and an adult pet cat continues this behaviour with its human owner. Those plaintive cries asking to be fed, let inside from the rain or demanding to be stroked are hard to ignore! Whatever delusions of grandeur your moggy may have, only a few large cats such as lions, tigers and leopards can roar.

It's very difficult to determine exactly when cats became domesticated because the skeletons of domestic cats and their wild predecessors are so similar. However, the skeleton of a domestic cat was found with its owner at an archeological site in Cyprus, having been buried about 9,500 years ago, so domestication must have occurred before then. Genetic studies suggest that cats began living with humans when agriculture blossomed in the Fertile Crescent of the Middle East around 12,000 years ago. Wildcats were probably attracted by the rodent pests that were drawn to our ancestors' grain stores and stayed to take advantage of this food source. No doubt, humans would have welcomed these cats if they helped to keep pests at bay. The origins of our pet cats are a bit murky but biologists suspect that their ancestors include the African and European wildcats, both subspecies of *Felis sylvestris* that might have interbred in the Middle East region.

Wildcats are found across Europe but in the UK they are restricted to Scotland where they are considered to be a unique subspecies, *Felis silvestris grampia*. They are superficially quite similar to our domestic cats and can interbreed with them, but their behaviour is quite different to that of a pet tabby that will sit on your knee. They are truly wild creatures and very elusive in their natural habitat.

Scottish wildcats lead a solitary life most of the time so, although they can make the same vocalisations as domestic cats, they generally remain silent. Instead they communicate by scent, marking their territories with faeces, urine or their scent glands. They only become vocal when they meet another cat during the breeding season or when they have kittens.

Most species of cat, large and small, can purr. Exactly how cats produce the purring sound is not yet understood entirely, but it is thought that the glottis (the area of the larynx with the vocal cords) is rapidly expanded and contracted as the cat breathes in and out, creating the characteristic vibration sounds. (We contract our glottis to create an 'h' sound in speech.) Unlike domestic cats, adult wildcats do not purr. Kittens purr from birth, especially when they are suckling, and purring is often interpreted to mean that the cat is content or happy. However, adult domestic cats sometimes purr during stressful situations or when they are in pain, perhaps as a means to comfort themselves or encourage others to provide care. Cats have learned that purring is a virtuous cycle – by showing pleasure they receive more pleasure, whether they are manipulating their mother or a cat-loving human.

Eggstatic

How can a tiny bird lay three or four eggs that have a total volume similar to that of themselves? *Lin*

Which bird lays the most eggs in one go? *Dicky*

Producing eggs requires a lot of effort and energy. In robins, for example, a complete clutch may be equivalent to 90 per cent of the female's body weight. During the laying period, female birds need to rest and eat extra calories – they often rely on their partner to bring them food. Each egg must be provided with a fat-rich yolk to feed the growing embryo, which is surrounded by egg white (albumen) and then encased in a calcium-rich shell. Not only is finding extra food and producing the eggs energetically costly but birds also have to raise their metabolic rate to generate enough warmth to incubate them.

Most songbirds lay just one egg per day while larger species such as swans or geese may have a one- or two-day interval between eggs. Eggs are heavy, and if the female retained them inside her body they would weigh her down, so as soon as an egg has formed it is laid. In the UK, the grey partridge has the largest clutch of any bird, usually 14–15 eggs in total, but they can lay up to 20 eggs. Clutches tend to be larger in species with chicks that can feed themselves soon after hatching, such as many waterfowl, while species whose chicks need more care and attention have smaller clutches. Many seabirds are long-lived and have just one egg per season, investing a lot of time and energy into feeding and raising a single chick.

Some birds, like great tits, have a single large clutch per year to coincide with a peak in food (caterpillars in the great tit's case), literally putting all their eggs in one basket. If the parents get the timing wrong or if their food supply fails they will have little breeding success. Other species, such as robins, spread their risk and can squeeze in two, three or even more clutches, especially if one brood fails, but have fewer eggs in each clutch.

The embryos inside fertilised eggs don't begin to develop until they are incubated by the parent. Some species, such as barn owls, start incubation as soon as the first egg is laid so the eggs hatch asynchronously over several days. This means that the first chicks are much larger than later ones and may even eat their younger siblings if food is scarce, as we saw on *Springwatch* with a barn owl chick named Hannibal. Most songbirds delay incubation until the clutch is complete, in which case all the eggs hatch at roughly the same time and the chicks are all a similar size. There may still be a runt of the clutch, because the final egg sometimes has fewer resources put into it, but generally each of these chicks has a more even chance of survival.

Make Mine a Double

I ate a double-yolk egg for my lunch. If it had been fertilised, would two chicks have grown/hatched from one egg? *Charlotte*

Double-yolk eggs are fairly rare – it's thought that about one in a thousand commercial hens' eggs have two yolks, and multiple yolks (triple, quadruple or more) are even rarer.

They are a result of a malfunction in the chicken's egg-laying process. Normally, an ovum is formed in the hen's ovary and develops into the yolk. When it reaches the right size it is released into the oviduct. On its journey through the oviduct, the egg white (albumen) and the shell form around the yolk to create a whole egg, which is then laid. The whole process takes about 24 hours and the laying of one egg usually triggers the ovulation of the next.

Egg formation and laying are regulated by the hen's hormones and occasionally things go wrong, especially in young hens. Two or more yolks may be released into the oviduct at the same time and become encased in one shell, resulting in a double-yolker.

Commercial eggs are unfertilised and do not develop into chicks. However, if domestic hens are kept with a cockerel and the eggs are fertilised then it's possible that a double-yolker would contain two chick embryos.

There are a few very rare cases where 'twin' chicks have hatched from a single fertilised egg, usually with human assistance. Generally, though, the embryos from a fertilised double-yolked egg would not survive as there simply isn't enough room in the egg for them to develop. Unlike mammals that have multiple embryos and a nice stretchy uterus, the eggshell cannot expand to accommodate more than one chick. Also, a chick has to be able to rotate within the egg so it can reach the air pocket in the round end, before pecking its way out. This would not be possible if two chicks were squeezed together into one shell. So fertilised double-yolkers are generally doomed but unfertilised ones make a great lunchtime bonus.

Hard-Headed

My eight-year-old daughter, Lauren, wants to know why a woodpecker doesn't break its beak when it hammers on a tree. *Jenny*

There are three species of woodpecker in the UK: the largest is the exotic-looking green woodpecker with its red crown and emerald plumage, often seen on the ground feeding on ants' nests. Green woodpeckers rarely drum, but the black-

and-white woodpecker species, the great spotted and lesser spotted, both hammer out their clarion call. During spring, these woodpeckers rapidly drum their beaks against trees, telegraph poles or even metal structures to attract a mate and claim their territory. They choose whichever substance will resonate and amplify their drumming the most.

Woodpeckers can strike their beaks up to 40 times per second, at a speed of 6 metres per second, and each time their beak hits the trunk it experiences a force of up to 1,000 times gravity. That's equivalent to a human hitting a wall face first at up to 22km/h, which would cause a nasty concussion, if not worse. So how does the woodpecker not get a headache or break its beak?

Fortunately, woodpeckers' beaks and skulls are well adapted to absorb the shockwaves and deal with those forces. Firstly, the brain fits very snugly into the skull so there is little room for it to bump around. Conversely, human brains are suspended in fluid and if we hit our heads the brain sloshes around, bouncing off the inside of the skull, which gives us concussion.

Secondly, the upper part of the woodpecker's beak is longer than the bottom half, which helps to disperse the forces. The beak can also be quite flexible so it changes shape as it hits the trunk and absorbs some of the impact. The bones of the skull are very spongy with a fine, mesh-like lining that acts as a shock absorber. Woodpeckers also have a special hyoid bone that loops around under the skull acting like a safety belt for the brain. These birds also have strong, thick neck muscles that support the head and power the drumming. All these adaptations are certainly put to the test during the breeding season, when a male looking for a mate may drum up to 600 times a day.

Follow Your Nose

Is it true that if released within a mile of your house, a mouse can navigate back? If so, how? Is it celestial navigation? *Kirsty from Lisburn, Northern Ireland*

Many animals have a strong homing instinct, used either during migration or simply to return home at night after a hard day's foraging. It makes sense that an animal must have a mental map to find its way around its home range or territory. House mice have variable home-range sizes depending on where they live and how much food is available. In a chicken barn with plenty of grain they may live in a tiny area of just four square metres; however, where house mice live out in the wild away from humans their home range may cover as much as one or two square kilometres. Most mice in homes will stay within an area less than 10 metres in diameter.

House mice are nocturnal and don't have colour vision. Their other senses more than compensate for their bad sight. Mice have good hearing and can detect ultrasonic sounds. They use their sensitive whiskers to find their way around in the dark. House mice exhibit 'thigmotaxis' which is a tendency to follow solid surfaces; for example, they prefer to run around the edge of a room, staying close to the wall, rather than run across open spaces. They use regular paths and runways to move around their patch, whether that's in a house or field. Mice also leave urine scent trails and spray landmarks around their territory. They are curious and constantly explore their home range using taste, smell and touch to memorise obstacles and where to find food and water.

As long as food is available, house mice have little cause to leave home, except when they are young and disperse to find their own territory. Some house mice have been recorded travelling up to 2.4 kilometres, but they usually don't roam that far.

So what happens if an animal is taken out of its local area and plonked in a strange new location, such as when a mouse is live-trapped and released well away from home? It seems that mice use various senses to navigate. Blind mice are worse at homing than sighted mice so vision must play a role. Mice are much better at homing if they are less than 135 metres from their original position. House mice don't tend to range very far so they may not need to be good at homing over large distances, but other species of mice that habitually travel across big areas of landscape are very adept at homing.

Experiments with deer mice (*Peromyscus maniculatus*) in North America showed that they could find their way home even if they were moved by up to two kilometres. How they navigate is uncertain. Some studies have suggested that certain species of mice might be able to detect the Earth's magnetic field with an internal compass, similar to migrating birds, while other researchers have found that voles may use the sun to navigate. Other biologists believe that mice may just wander extensively if lost and eventually find their way home by luck rather than judgement. Despite the conflicting evidence, homeowners are still advised to release any mice that they trap well away from their house (or any other houses for that matter!); some pest controllers recommend relocating the mice up to a distance of 3.2 kilometres. The best bet is to try to prevent house mice entering your home by sealing up any access points, especially where food is kept. Bird food kept in a shed or garage can attract rodents so it is wise to keep any nuts, seeds, etc. in sealed tubs or bins that are tough enough to withstand sharp little teeth.

Hello Mum

I believe baby birds imprint on the first thing they see as they emerge from the egg. So how does the cuckoo find a mate when they are raised by surrogate parents that are usually smaller, looking nothing like a likely mate?
Nick

There are several types of imprinting in chicks. The behaviour that Nick refers to is called filial imprinting, in which a young bird becomes very attached to a particular object soon after hatching, usually its parent. This is vital for birds such as geese, ducks and other waterfowl and waders that leave the nest shortly after hatching. If a chick is to survive it must follow and stay with its parent. Hatchlings from artificially incubated eggs will latch on to whatever they see during the critical imprinting period, whether it is another animal, human, or even an inanimate object, because the instinct is so strong.

There is evidence that some birds also experience sexual imprinting, learning from their parent's appearance how future mates should look and sound. In essence, a chick learns to recognise members of its own species so that later in life it can court and mate with its own kind. This process would be disastrous for a cuckoo, though, because it is brought up in the nest of another species such as a reed warbler, dunnock or meadow pipit.

Cuckoos are brood parasites and rely on parents of the host species to bring up their chicks. Female cuckoos wait for a suitable nest to be left unattended before flying down, removing one of the host's eggs and replacing it with one of her own. She can lay the egg and make a quick getaway in about 10 seconds. When the unsuspecting parents return they incubate the cuckoo egg and raise the chick as their own. The cuckoo chick usually hatches first and ejects all the other eggs or chicks from the nest, ensuring it has no rivals for its surrogate parents' attention. Meanwhile the cuckoo parents return to Africa and never see their chicks. Instead, the host parents work tirelessly to feed the enormous chick, which can grow to over three times their own size. When the cuckoo finally fledges, it must find its own way to Africa. In the cuckoo's case, the ability to migrate must be genetically hard-wired in the brain and is innate rather than learned.

But how does a cuckoo avoid sexual imprinting on the wrong species and know that it is a cuckoo rather than a reed warbler or a dunnock? Biologists aren't entirely sure how cuckoos learn to recognise a mate and there may be several processes at work. Perhaps some innate elements are later reinforced by mixing with other cuckoos. Brown-headed cowbirds, which use the same breeding strategy as cuckoos, have been shown to use a species-specific 'password' to trigger their learning. They make a particular chatter call when they join up after fledging and then learn more about their species. They also look to themselves and reference their own traits, such as 'that bird looks like me so probably belongs to the same species'. Cuckoos are likely to have a similar system for working out their own identity and recognising which birds are potential mates.

Awkward Embrace

We noticed one of our smallish koi carp desperately flipping and trying to free itself from what looked like a black 'growth' around its head and gills. We netted the fish and discovered a large toad had it tightly in its grasp. My husband forced the toad off the exhausted fish, which has now recovered in a bucket. The toad jumped back into the pond where there are more fish! We've never seen this before. Was the toad trying to 'mate' with the fish? *Jill, Sussex*

In essence, yes, the koi carp was on the receiving end of an overexcited toad's amorous attentions! As soon as night-time temperatures reach 5 degrees Celsius or more, usually in February, adult common toads emerge from hibernation. They have just one thing on their mind: mating. They migrate back to their ancestral pond, often travelling several kilometres and crossing dangerous, busy roads. The males often arrive before the females and will lie in wait, either at the pond itself or nearby, ready to pounce on a potential mate. The smaller male will often piggyback on the larger female as she makes her way to the water.

The male grasps tightly onto the female under the armpits in a special hold called amplexus, Latin for 'embrace'. During the breeding season the male develops 'nuptial pads' on his first three fingers that help him grip onto the female. Males are so intent on breeding that they will often grab toads of the wrong sex or even completely different species like the unfortunate koi carp. Males usually outnumber females at the breeding ponds and competition for mates is high, so it makes sense to grab anything that moves and ask questions later! Actually, males aren't even that choosy, and have been known to latch on to inanimate objects while in their aroused state.

Male toads will croak their objections loudly if grabbed by mistake, and usually the grabber will let go within a few seconds. Fish can't be so vocal, though, and there would have been no audible cue to encourage the confused toad to release Jill's fish. It was lucky that Jill's husband spotted the embrace when he did, otherwise the koi carp may have endured a long struggle. Male toads are persistent and will often hang on to the female for several days. One female may attract the attentions of several males, resulting in a writhing orgy of warty skin and interlocked limbs – who'd be a female toad?! Eventually the strongest male will be successful and will fertilise the female's eggs as she lays them, up to 6,000 eggs in long double strings.

One study found that 80 per cent of males returned to the pond where they were spawned, so it's likely that Jill's toad was a tadpole in her pond, perhaps before it was stocked with fish. Toads can be long-lived and lucky individuals may reach up to 40 years old, so it might be worth keeping an eye out for this overzealous toad for a few years to come.

Confusing Courtship

The males and females of some birds, such as robins, look identical. So how does a male robin know he is chatting up a female robin, and not another fella? And why do they both have red breasts? *Sue*

Many birds are sexually dimorphic – that is, the male and female look very different. Usually, the males are the more colourful, showy sex and females tend to be more drab. Perhaps the most extreme example of this is the peacock, with its magnificent blue-green tail that creates a dazzling fan. However, familiar British birds such as grouse, blackbirds and many species of duck, such as mallards, also have males that are more eye-catching than the females. Other birds have more subtle cues, such as the yellower chests of male blue tits that are particularly apparent when viewed in ultraviolet light, which birds, unlike humans, can detect.

In 1859 Charles Darwin first proposed that male birds used elaborate plumage to impress females in his book *On the Origin of Species*. He argued that the males evolved ornaments such as beautiful feathers, or beguiling courtship rituals like the complex dances performed by birds of paradise, to woo the females, which then choose their partners according to their fitness. At the time, Darwin's entire theory of evolution was controversial and met with much consternation, but the concept of female choice was especially scandalous at a time when women had little control over their lives in a patriarchal Victorian society.

Anyway, back to robins! Robins are unusual because both males and females hold territories throughout the year and defend them vigorously. Their red chest feathers act as a warning to other robins rather than an attraction to potential mates. The male and female both have bright orange/red breasts that stand out amid the gloom of dusk and dawn when they are often active. They use their beautiful song and brilliant red chests to see off any intruders. A robin will find a high perch, fluff out the feathers to show as much red as possible then sing out its melodious war song. If the vivid red chest is their war paint, then their song is their battle cry.

Most of the time, the opponent submits and a fight is avoided. If not, the owner will attack, and may even peck the other bird to death. Up to 10 per cent of robins might die in this way. Robins are so feisty that any object of a similar colour may be attacked, like the apocryphal red rag to a bull. We've had reports of assaults on orange lawnmowers, red socks and even someone gardening in a red jumper.

From late December onwards, the robin's thoughts turn to romance, but courtship can be confusing when both sexes look almost the same. The male may be a little brighter and slightly larger than the female but even robins may have difficulty telling the sexes apart. They have to take into account how a robin acts rather than rely on how it looks. During the breeding season, females approach their chosen male's territory with care. Sometimes, the male mistakes his lover for a fighter and initially responds aggressively, singing at the 'intruder'. She patiently listens and doesn't sing back – instead she follows him around. After a few hours, her patience pays off and he finally accepts her. They set up home together and both fiercely defend their patch. Robins may look cute and appealing but they are gutsy little warriors.

Topsy Turvy

How do bats hang upside for so long without any adverse effects, such as poor blood circulation? *The Chameleon*

Bats spend the daylight hours hanging upside down in a secluded spot, such as the roof of a cave or the inside of a hollow tree, safely hidden away from predators and inclement weather. Hanging up high has another advantage: bats can't run and launch into flight like birds can; instead they drop into the air straight into flight.

Their bodies have a number of adaptations to deal with this topsy-turvy lifestyle. For example, they have specially adapted feet for hanging upside down. If we want to grip onto something with our hands we use our muscles to close our fingers around it, but the tendons in bats' feet and legs work the opposite way round. Bats have to flex muscles to open their grip, and the talons shut when they relax. The weight of the bat locks the foot into a tight but effortless clasp. This means bats don't use any energy when they hang upside down and their grip remains constant, even after death.

In most mammals, the knees bend forwards. This would be awkward for bats hanging against a surface, and their knees bend the other way. Many bats have a flap of skin between the legs which they use to catch bugs, and their backward-bending knees form a basket to hold their prey. Bats' respiratory and cardiovascular systems are also adapted for the high energetic demands of flight. The heart is up to three times as large as that of a non-flying mammal of a similar size and they can increase their heart rate up to 1,000 beats per minute when flying.

Bats are also much smaller and lighter than us so they don't experience the blood rush to the head that we would when hanging upside down. We have evolved to live upright and our circulation system reflects that. Our circulation system has one-way valves that prevent blood pooling in our feet and legs. Conversely, a bat's large, powerful heart and specialised valves in its blood vessels prevent any blood pooling in its head. Evidently, bats have overcome any downsides to gravity as they can remain hanging upside down for weeks during hibernation with no adverse effects.

Feeling Sleepy?

Is it just mammals that yawn or do all animals yawn?
Helks

Yawning isn't unique to humans or even mammals but there can be confusion over what constitutes a yawn. Animals may show their wide-open mouths in a variety of situations. This is not necessarily a yawn but may be a gape. Opening the mouth fully can be part of a threat display used to show off fearsome teeth, such as in baboons. Birds may display open beaks during a courtship display.

A 'real' yawn is usually involuntary and starts with a large intake of breath, stretching the mouth wide, and then an exhalation. If the yawn is accompanied by a good stretch then it is delightfully known as 'pandiculation'. Most vertebrates appear to do this to some degree. Despite being such a widespread behaviour and one that we experience regularly there is no obvious reason for or benefit of yawning. Yawning is seen as a sign of boredom or tiredness, but why would either of those states instigate a great, big yawn?

One long-held theory is that yawning is triggered by a lack of oxygen or a build-up of carbon dioxide – taking a large breath counteracts this by drawing in oxygen and expelling carbon dioxide. This seems to be hot air though. In experiments, increasing the levels of carbon dioxide or oxygen in a controlled atmosphere had little effect on how often people yawned. Another idea is that yawning is used to cool the brain. Yawning seems to be suppressed by an ice pack on the forehead or when the air is warmer than body temperature. Yet neither of these theories can account for why unborn babies yawn in the womb – even an eleven-week-old foetus has been shown to yawn. Yawning does appear to increase blood flow to the brain (the heart rate may increase) and promote alertness.

Have you yawned yet? One thing we do know about yawning is that it is highly contagious. It's almost impossible to restrain a yawn once you've seen someone else yawning and even reading about it can trigger the reflex. This has led some biologists to believe that contagious yawning, is a sign of empathy, the ability to understand someone else's state of mind and emotions. People with less developed empathy, such as children under about four years old and those with autism, don't find yawning so contagious.

Yawning may have evolved to be contagious as a form of social bonding or group communication. A few other species also find yawning infectious and both chimpanzees and dogs that live in social groups will yawn in response to others. One theory is that this would allow the group to synchronise their rest periods or increase general alertness to compensate for one member's tiredness. It just goes to show that there is plenty left to discover about human and animal behaviour, even with something as seemingly straightforward as a yawn.

Old Sparrow, New Tricks

How long do sparrows live? A few years ago, a male sparrow visiting the seed feeder in our yard was seen flying to the top of our wall with seeds for his fledglings for a few days, then the next day, when they were able to fly down to the ground, he perched at the feeder and dropped seed to them. He then seemed to get fed up with this process because it was too slow, so took to flying at the feeder and crashing into it with both feet up to shake a shower of seed down. The next year, we saw the same behaviour but then not for the next couple of years. So when it reappeared this year we wondered if it could be the same bird, or one of his descendants. Any ideas? *Linda*

Linda doesn't mention whether the sparrow was a tree or house sparrow but either way it's likely that the clever parenting she witnessed was performed by two different birds. The oldest recorded house sparrow lived for twelve years but their average lifespan is about three years. A tree sparrow is known to have lived for over ten years but typically they only survive for a couple of years. So, while it's feasible that the original sparrow returned, it is unlikely. Instead, the new feeder-bashing sparrow could be evidence of an interesting phenomenon called cultural learning.

Cultural learning occurs when a new behaviour, like a novel feeding strategy, is transmitted from one individual to another within a population or from one generation to the next. This is particularly important in social birds such as house sparrows and starlings. Recent research suggests that birds living in large groups, such as sparrows, are better at solving problems because the individuals all have different experiences and skills to draw upon. We'll never know whether Sue's feeder-bashing sparrows learned the trick from the original sparrow or worked it out independently. However, if the behaviour had been passed on it doesn't imply that the original feeder-bashing sparrow intentionally taught the new skill to others; they probably just imitated him.

The most well-known instance of cultural learning is the intriguing case of the milk thieves. In the good old days, when milk was delivered to the doorstep by a friendly milkman whistling a merry tune, an inquisitive blue tit or great tit discovered that those glass bottles contained fat-rich cream. Originally, milk was delivered in open bottles that birds could easily drink from, but later, when milk bottles were covered with silver foil, blue tits and great tits soon learned to peck through the foil to steal the creamy goodness underneath. The pecking of milk bottle tops rapidly became widespread. It took 25 years for the habit to grow from one observation to being seen in over 400 different locations. Whether each bird worked out how to do this independently or just watched and copied others is open to debate. The behaviour did not spread out in a wave from the original location but popped up sporadically, suggesting that it arose on several occasions. Blue tits and great tits often peel off bark looking for insects and grubs. They are naturally curious and have relatively large brains so it would not have been a huge step to try peeling off milk bottle tops. Of course, there's no reason why birds would not have copied the behaviour from each other within each location, so it's likely that a combination of inquisitive individuals and social learning was responsible for the stolen milk. Now that fewer people have milk delivered, this behaviour is rarely seen.

Run, Rabbit, Run

Why do rabbits have white, furry bottoms? Does this not make them easier for predators to spot? *Lupodod*

Rabbits certainly have their fair share of predators. Fully-grown rabbits are taken by foxes, cats, stoats and polecats while young rabbits are preyed on by badgers, buzzards and weasels. Over 90 per cent of baby rabbits die in the first year of life, most of these in the first three months. Some may die of disease, but a huge number are eaten. This high mortality rate is the main reason why rabbits are so fecund and, well, breed like rabbits! The female can have two or three litters per year, giving birth to about ten young each time. Producing lots of young increases the chance that some will make it through to adulthood and successfully reproduce.

As they are on the menu of so many predators, rabbits are very vigilant, constantly on the lookout for danger. They have eyes set wide on the sides of their skull which give them a broad field of vision, and sit on their hind legs to see further.

With so many enemies around, it might seem counter-intuitive for a prey animal like a rabbit to make itself more visible by having a white rump. However, the white underside of a rabbit's stubby tail (called a scut) is not that easy to see when the rabbit is grazing or moving slowly. It's most noticeable when the rabbit is running, probably heading away from danger. This has led to several theories why rabbits have white tails.

Firstly, it acts as a warning to other rabbits in the warren. If a rabbit senses danger it raises its tail and thumps its foot to alert other members of the warren. Rabbits are mostly active in the low light conditions of dawn and dusk so a white flash would stand out, alerting other rabbits to run. Another theory suggests that by having a white tail, predators are attracted to the 'right' end of the rabbit and aim for the rear instead of the head, giving the rabbit a greater chance of escaping.

Rabbits also have a strict hierarchy and there can be a lot of aggression within the colony. Males, called bucks, will fight for access to females, known as does. The most dominant buck gains mating rights while the does compete for nest sites. Fights between the females can lead to serious injuries and even death. So one theory suggests that the tails are used like a white flag in surrender, to show submission to other rabbits and avoid potentially deadly fights. Dominant rabbits tend to be caught by predators more often than those lower in the hierarchy, perhaps because they are distracted by fights or because chasing off other rabbits makes their white tails more visible.

The rabbit's tail probably has several functions, but the costs of having a white, fluffy bottom must be outweighed by the benefits or natural selection would have led to something a bit less conspicuous.

Pitching Up

I was driving to Brecon in south Wales last week and saw several colonies of tent-making caterpillars. The colonies were all very large, a metre or so long. Some of the colonies had completely stripped the hedgerow for long stretches and all that was left was twigs and silk. Are these native to the UK (I have seen very much smaller colonies on hawthorn) or are they an invasive species?
Rob

There are quite a few native species of moths and butterflies whose caterpillars make tents, such as the lackey moth (*Malacosoma neustria*) and marsh fritillary butterfly (*Euphydryas aurinia*). However, the impressive size and extent of the tents that Rob describes suggests that they were made by one of our eight species of ermine moth that belong to the genus *Yponomeuta*.

The adult moths are fairly inconspicuous, with white or grey wings adorned with rows of black spots and a wingspan of 15–26 millimetres, depending on the species. The caterpillars and their webs are much more noticeable, though, especially when there's a population explosion and their numbers grow to epic proportions. This can occur when there is a lack of predators or parasites (ermine caterpillars are often parasitised by ichneumon wasps) or when weather conditions work in their favour. The caterpillars' fleecy white tents can cover large areas of trees and hedgerows, looking like giant spider's webs or something out of a horror film. The truth is much less sinister.

Each ermine species has a favoured host food plant on which eggs are laid and the caterpillars subsequently munch their way through. For example, the colonies that Rob saw on hawthorn were probably caterpillars of the small or orchard ermine moth (*Yponomeuta padella*). The adults are on the wing in June/July and the females lay clusters of eggs on their specific food plant. These hatch into tiny larvae that spend the winter burrowed into leaves or stems. They emerge in spring when the buds burst and turn into busy eating machines. A caterpillar grows quickly until it literally needs to burst out of its skin in a process called ecdysis. Once it reaches a certain size, a caterpillar sheds its skin so that it can grow into the next stage, or instar. Most moth and butterfly caterpillars go through this four or five times, and a caterpillar can grow to over a thousand times heavier than when it emerged from the egg.

Ermine moth caterpillars live in large groups and construct their characteristic tents from silk. They bind leaves together in loose webs and feed on the leaves within them or nearby. As they run out of leaves, the caterpillars extend the tents to cover new areas of tree or bush. If the caterpillars venture beyond the safety of the web, they can leave a trail of chemical pheromones to find their way back.

The tents provide protection from predators – few birds would risk getting caught up in the silken webs. The layers of silk also act as insulation, retaining heat and encouraging the caterpillars to remain huddled together. The caterpillars need warmth for their digestion to work efficiently. Once they have grown large enough, the caterpillar will pupate and transform into an adult moth.

The plants that the caterpillars feed on may be stripped of leaves. Some ermine moth caterpillars can be minor agricultural pests but generally the plants affected soon recover. After all, it wouldn't be in the moths' interest for the caterpillars to destroy their host plant as they will be returning as adults a few weeks later to lay their own eggs on it.

Spring Quiz

1. If you were offered a plate of wallfish, what would you be eating?

      A. Crayfish
      B. Wild strawberries
      C. Garden snails
      D. Mussels

2. Spring sees the arrival of many of our migrant birds, but which travels the furthest?

      A. Swallow
      B. Swift
      C. Osprey
      D. Arctic tern

3. Which of the following reptiles lay eggs?

      A. Adder
      B. Common lizard
      C. Grass snake
      D. Slowworm

4. A flock of goldfinches is delightfully known as a 'charm', but which animals gather in these more ominous-sounding groups?

  A. An unkindness
  B. A siege
  C. A smack
  D. A scream

5. If a dog is described as canine, which animal is vulpine?

  A. A vole
  B. A fox
  C. A peregrine falcon
  D. A red squirrel

6. Which iconic spring flower is also known as the Lent lily?

  A. Wild daffodil
  B. Primrose
  C. Wild garlic
  D. Bluebell

Spring Quiz Answers

Question 1 Answer:

C. Wallfish is a traditional name for garden snails.

Question 2 Answer:

D. Despite their name, Arctic terns fly from the Antarctic pack ice 20,000 kilometres away and have the longest recorded migration of any bird on the planet. Swallows arrive from South Africa about 9,500 kilometres from the UK, swifts return from spending the winter in central Africa about 6,500 kilometres away and ospreys migrate more than 5,000 kilometres from west Africa.

Question 3 Answer:

C. Only grass snakes lay eggs. Adders, slowworms and common lizards are all ovoviviparous; that is, they incubate their eggs internally and give birth to live young. The babies are encased in a membranous egg sac that they break out of during or soon after birth.

Question 4 Answer:

A. Ravens (also known as a conspiracy of ravens – equally scheming!)

B. Herons

C. Jellyfish

D. Swifts

Question 5 Answer:

B. A fox, from the Latin name *Vulpes vulpes*

Question 6 Answer:

A. The wild daffodil, *Narcissus pseudonarcissus*, is known as the Lent lily because its yellow trumpets bloom in early spring and are usually finished by Easter.

Summer

Elderflower cordial – that's the taste of summer! – those blousey heads of elderflower blossom, swaying in the breeze, epitomising the explosion of lush new growth that comes in early summer.

Swallows will be busy nesting by now, but sickle-shaped swifts, the most aerial of all birds, only start to nest once summer is underway. When a baby swift tumbles out from its nest and opens its wings, taking to the air for the very first time, it does not touch the ground again for at least two years. That's two years of ceaseless flight; drinking on the wing, feeding on the wing, and never once touching the ground. I was once lazily watching a village cricket match and saw an odd-looking swift gliding towards me – what was wrong with it? To my delight, the single swift suddenly transformed into two swifts – I had actually witnessed swifts mating on the wing. Just imagine how odd it must feel when they touch down for the first time, after two years in the air, finally having to use their tiny legs to try to move on solid ground. After two years of minimal use, swifts' nails are very long and sharp, making them one of the bird-ringers' least favourite birds to work with!

Swifts were traditionally known as devil birds due to their unearthly screams, but to me this sound is another essence of summer, a magical noise. Swifts are a joy to watch as they sweep in, impossibly fast, and dive under roofs to nest, even in the middle of town. I once had to stop my motorbike in the middle of Glastonbury to watch swifts coming and going under the eves of one house. These are birds that think nothing of travelling hundreds of miles in search of a good meal, riding along the storm fronts, climbing high to glean aerial plankton and then moving in great curving arcs at dusk as they snatch sleep on the wing.

There's so much to see and do in summer – here are a few ideas to help you get the most of this fascinating season, ranging from easy to perhaps more challenging.

A simple summer thrill is setting up a moth trap. You can spend money and buy a trap off the shelf or, as I did as a child, use a bit of wire and a pillowcase tied up around an outside light. Each morning there will be a thrilling collection of exotic moths (and probably other things too) to delight the eye and stimulate the mind. Some moth names are absolutely splendid, 'Kentish glory', 'the small chocolate tip', 'scarlet tiger', 'dingy footman', 'heart and dart', 'true lover's knot', 'the hedge rustic', 'scarce burnished brass', 'beautiful golden Y', 'pale brindled beauty', 'tawny speckled pug' – and a personal favourite, the 'Setaceous Hebrew character!'. I mean, who made up these names? There is actually a whole network of 'moth twitchers' who, like bird watchers, keep in contact and share notes about what they have found. Some moths migrate in huge numbers from Africa to the UK, so you can see some exotic specimens in summer, for example, some years well over 200 million 'Silver Y' moths arrive in the UK in the summer months, travelling at altitude to catch high-speed northerly winds. Moths have been timed travelling up to 90 km/h during wind-assisted migration and can travel 700 kilometres in a single flight.

From the fast and exotic to the more down to earth and slow ... If you have snails in the garden (big garden snails are best), try this. Make a solution of sugar water, wipe a bit on a window pane, then offer your snail up to the glass and sugar solution until it attaches itself. Go around the other side of the glass and watch the snail feed – it's a strange sight, the hard dark mouthparts, the 'radula', working away hoovering up the sugar water. You will also see the way the muscular 'foot' works from underneath. It is curiously mesmerising, and obviously kids love this.

Talking of kids, rock pooling with them in summer is brilliant, but I have just discovered something even better. Whilst filming in Dorset for *Springwatch* we happened across a 'snorkel trail'. You start on the beach then gently swim out to the first of five marker buoys. At the first buoy you look down and explore a sandy habitat, with perhaps sand eels and a young plaice, then you move on to the second buoy, which is now a glorious kelp forest, then an anemone garden, and so on. Each buoy marks a different marine habitat. The snorkel trail is carefully set up each year around May (weather permitting) and you get a waterproof card to take with you to tell you what you might see. It's all just off shore in Kimmeridge Bay. It is a genius idea! This summer I'm going to do the trail myself.

Along with us holiday makers, around 8 million seabirds visit the coast of the UK to nest each year. It is one of the greatest gatherings of wildlife anywhere on Earth and it's a doddle to go and see – well, some of it is. There are gigantic nesting colonies on sea cliffs all around the UK, one of my favourites is Bempton, which is sandwiched between Scarborough and Bridlington on the Yorkshire coast. Around 200,000 birds nest on the chalk cliffs here and you can just wander over to watch them with an ice cream in your hand – it's that easy. Of course there are other sea cliffs that are for the perhaps more intrepid wildlife watcher: Skomer Island in Wales, Bass Rock (with the largest nesting colony of northern gannets in the world), Orkney, Shetland and Fair Isle off the northern tip of Scotland. Why not have a real summer adventure?

By the way, if you're in Shetland you could go whale watching. Simon King and I watched a pod of mighty killer whales hunting seals just off the shore in Shetland, an unforgettable sight. Whale watching is a thrilling summer pastime to consider. If you go to the east coast of Ireland you can watch many different species of dolphins and whales, including, remarkably, 35-ton humpbacks who may be breaching, hurling themselves almost out of the water before falling back with an enormous splash. To many people's surprise, humpback whales are regularly found in waters around the UK in summer, but they have to go south to warmer waters in autumn in order to give birth. They are warm blooded after all, and the Irish Sea is too cold for a newborn baby whale (even if it is 13-foot long and weighs in at around 2 tons!).

If, like me, you are interested in insects and other small animals the OPAL initiative ('Open Air laboratory' – run by a group of 15 different universities and institutions) have some really well organised surveys for you to do (www.opalexplorenature.org/aboutOPAL), but bear in mind that these are also surveys with a serious scientific purpose, analysing insect populations to help us understand what is happening to our crucial pollinators, for instance. OPAL surveys always have fantastic downloadable picture identification guides (I would have hoarded them as a child!). The FSC (Field Studies Council) guides are absolutely gorgeous too – laminated, very tough and inexpensive. Every home should have some.

Be careful! Insect collecting and identifying can become an overriding passion. In the Natural History Museum insect collections there are some beetles with the following label: 'Dead tramp, New Forest, A. M. Massie'. Massie was a well-known beetle collector, so when he and a friend came across a dead tramp they seized the opportunity and, taking one end each, shook him gently to see what beetles fell out. Sure enough, beetles did appear – sexton beetles, so-called because they bury dead animals to provide food for their developing young. Some very ambitious beetles were having a go at getting the tramp underground! As with all exciting hobbies, there is a danger that you can take things just that little bit too far.

You can help insects (and lots of other wildlife) by leaving a bit of your garden or allotment rough and ready – don't tidy it up too much, neat is not good for wildlife spotting. It may need to be left 'wild' for a good time, as stag beetles, for instance, can spend seven years as larvae feeding on rotting wood before they emerge as adults, in all their tawny magnificence. Advice on stag beetles and how to build a 'loggery' can be found at: www.lbp.org.uk/downloads/Publications/Management/stag_advice.pdf.

The special 'Unsprung' word for summer is 'apophallation'. Slugs are hermaphrodite, with both male and female organs. Sometimes their complex penises get so entangled during mating that they cannot separate, so the slugs simply bite them off. This is 'apophallation'. No comment!

One final thought, the easiest method of all for lazy but keen wildlife watchers is using web cameras. There are now web cams set up all over the country, which means you can watch the most intimate and fascinating moments in animals' lives on your computer, as they happen. Some excellent web cam footage can be viewed at: www.wildlifetrusts.org/webcams. I can't believe I can sit up in bed with a cuppa, watching the comings and goings in a peregrine's nest which is set dizzyingly high up on top of a church in Bath or a university building in Nottingham. Technology is allowing us unparalleled access to the natural world from the comfort of our own homes.

Deadly Babies

I sometimes see baby adders while walking my dogs on Witley Common, Surrey. Can you please tell me if adders are born venomous or whether they obtain venom at 'puberty'? *Rosemary*

Firstly, well spotted! Adders are secretive creatures and their zigzag markings make excellent camouflage so they're not easy to see.

The adder is the UK's only venomous snake. Females give birth to live young in August and September and can produce up to 20 babies, each about 16–18 centimetres long, roughly the size and shape of an earthworm. That's quite a feat considering that adult females rarely grow longer than a metre! The baby adders stay with their mother for a few days but she doesn't appear to take much care of them. And, yes, the young are born with fully functioning venom, ready to hunt and fend for themselves.

Adder's venom contains two types of toxin: haemotoxins that attack the circulation system (heart and blood), and cytotoxins that break down cells in tissue near the bite. The venom is used to immobilise their prey, mostly lizards, amphibians, chicks and small mammals. After striking, the adder waits for the venom to take effect before following the victim's scent to track down the body and swallow it whole. This hunting method means adders don't have to struggle with their prey, minimising their risk of injury.

Adders get a bad press but they'll only bite humans in self-defence or when provoked. About 100 people are bitten by adders each year in Britain, mostly in the summer. Owing to their inconspicuous nature, people can tread on adders by mistake, but half of the people treated are bitten on the hand while trying to pick one up. So to avoid being bitten, wear sturdy boots in areas where adders are known to live, keep your eyes peeled and don't try to handle them. If you are unlucky enough to be bitten, seek medical attention immediately. Bites are painful but rarely serious unless they trigger an anaphylactic reaction – only 14 people are known to have died as a result of an adder bite since records began in 1876; the most recent case was reported in 1975.

Inquisitive dogs are much more likely to be bitten than people and, as they're smaller than us, an adder's venom can have a much greater effect. If you suspect your dogs have been bitten by an adder, take them straight to the vet for treatment. You can reduce the chance of your dogs being bitten by keeping them on a lead between March and October in areas where there are adders. As a bonus, this will also prevent disturbing ground-nesting birds such as nightjars.

As long as you take sensible precautions for yourself and your dogs, there's no reason why you shouldn't continue to enjoy watching these beautiful animals.

Tadpole Tardiness

I'd like to know why the tadpoles in my pond are 'stuck' at the large tadpole stage and don't seem to be developing into little frogs? *Shirley from Cheltenham*

I have a small pond in my garden and had frogspawn in early spring. They are still tadpoles with no legs. Please can you explain why? This has happened for the last couple of years. *Sue*

Usually, tadpoles completely transform or 'metamorphose' into small frogs over the course of 12 to 16 weeks and are ready to leave the pond in the summer. But it's fairly common for tadpoles to stop developing if they don't have exactly the right conditions. There can be several reasons for this. Frogs will lay spawn in pools less than a metre across, and if a pond is small, like Sue's, it may be overcrowded so there won't be enough food for all the tadpoles to grow. Don't be tempted to move spawn or tadpoles to another pond, though, as this may spread diseases. Over time, the number of tadpoles in your pond will reach a natural balance. It sounds harsh, but that's why frogs lay so much spawn – it's part of their survival strategy. Roughly one in fifty eggs will survive to the froglet stage and on average only one in 400 eggs will make it to adulthood.

Temperature affects metamorphosis too. Tadpoles are poikilothermic (cold-blooded) animals, which means that their bodies are at the same temperature as their surroundings. If the pond is shaded or has steep sides then the water might be too cold for development – you could try cutting back any overhanging plants that are casting shade and try to provide shallow areas that will warm up in the sun. Even if you have a large pond in a sunny position, tadpoles may grow slowly if the weather is cold.

Attempts to feed the tadpoles and help them grow aren't advisable either. Providing extra food at this stage could lead to the tadpoles completing their development in the middle of winter, which means they'd end up leaving the pond at a time when there are few natural sources of food in the garden to support them.

So don't worry, the tadpoles will probably overwinter in their current state and then continue to develop into frogs next spring. There is even evidence to suggest that this may be a deliberate strategy for some frogs. Tadpoles that overwinter and don't develop into frogs until the following spring can metamorphose at a larger size and may have an advantage over smaller tadpoles that complete their development in one year. Maybe Sue just has canny tadpoles!

Feathers Count

This is something I've wondered for years ... My dad always used to joke, 'There's forty fousand fevvers on a frush', but how many feathers are there really on a bird? Does a blue tit have the same number as a kestrel except that the feathers vary in size – or does a kestrel have hundreds more? *Skylark Sue*

As Sue suggests, the number of feathers on a bird does vary according to their size, but it also depends on the species and season. Sue's dad was wrong, though; most songbirds have between 1,500 and 4,000 feathers. Nobody has ever counted, but the British Trust for Ornithology estimates that a thrush is covered in about 3,000 feathers. So, it would be more accurate to say, 'there's free fousand feathers on a frush'!

As a general rule, the bigger the bird, the more feathers it has. The lowest recorded number is 940 feathers on a ruby hummingbird and the highest is 25,216 on a whistling swan – hats off to whoever counted them all! But counting each feather would be the only way to work it out, as there's no simple equation to say that a particular bird has X square centimetres of skin so will have Y number of feathers. That's because feathers provide vital insulation and small birds, which are particularly vulnerable to heat loss, have more feathers per unit area of skin than bigger ones, to help retain warmth. Many birds also have more feathers in winter for added insulation.

Feathers aren't evenly distributed all over the body; instead they grow in distinct lines, or tracts, called pterylae, with areas of bare skin in between called apteria. These bare patches help the bird regulate its temperature: too hot and it can expose them, too cold and the bird covers them up. As you might expect, species that live in cold conditions, such as waterfowl, have much less bare skin and penguins have hardly any.

During the nesting season, many birds develop brood patches (bare patches of skin with plenty of blood vessels near the surface), usually on the breast. When the parent bird sits on eggs or chicks, the brood patch acts like a radiator, keeping the young warm. Most species shed their feathers automatically during the breeding season, but ducks and geese may pluck their own bellies and use the feathers to line their nest. Feathers soon grow back and cover the brood patch as the young become independent.

Birds' heads are particularly susceptible to heat loss. Usually, 30–40 per cent of a bird's feathers are found on the head and neck to protect the brain from extremes of temperature, so it's actually rather a good idea to be feather brained!

Carrier Bats?

I am curious to know what female bats do with their babies when they hunt. I know they are mammals and the babies are milk-fed, but do they carry them, or just hang them up somewhere? *Susie*

Compared to other animals of a similar size, bats are the slowest-reproducing mammals on Earth. Females do not breed until they are a couple of years old and then they may not breed every year. Most of the 16 species of British bat give birth to a single baby and they look after it very carefully. In contrast, a harvest mouse, which weighs roughly the same, has up to seven litters a year, each with up to eight babies. They have very different life strategies – harvest mice produce many babies that live fast and die young with a maximum lifespan of 18 months in the wild. At the other extreme, a greater horseshoe bat can live up to 30 years and invest heavily in each pup.

Baby bats are huge compared to their mother – they can weigh up to 40 per cent of her body weight, equivalent to a human mother giving birth to a baby the size of a five-year-old child (ouch!). Pregnant females gather in late May and early June to form maternity or nursery roosts in buildings, trees or caves where they have their pups communally. Despite their size, the babies are bald and very vulnerable – they can't regulate their own temperature and are completely dependent on their mother's milk.

Growing such a large baby and producing milk requires many calories. Pipistrelles can eat up to 3,000 small insects, such as gnats and mosquitoes, per night. Lactating females need to go out foraging to replenish their energy and they will usually leave the babies hanging up, often clustered together for warmth. They'll return every few hours so the babies can suckle. Mothers can carry their babies while they're still small, if necessary; for example, if the baby falls or the roost is disturbed and they need to move to a safer location. Horseshoe bats even have an extra pair of false nipples that provide additional 'handles' for the babies to hang on to. The babies suckle until they are ready to fly and hunt for themselves, at about five to six weeks old.

On the Edge

I have been following the progress of four peregrine falcon chicks on the webcam set up at Nottingham Trent University. The young birds are losing their downy feathers at a rapid rate and are exploring their surroundings, venturing onto the ledge high above the city. My question is, how do young birds which nest on cliffs know when it is safe to attempt their first flight, or are there instances of overconfident birds falling to their death? *Malcolm*

There are a few challenges for cliff-nesting birds such as peregrines, kittiwakes and gulls, and these are particularly clear when they move into cities. The dangers of nesting in a precarious position have to be outweighed by the safety of bring up young in an inaccessible place away from most predators. The eggs of these species are specially adapted for small ledges – their conical shape means they swivel in a tight circle, lessening their chance of falling off the edge. But once those chicks have hatched and are ready to leave the nest, there aren't many second chances when it comes to fledging from a sheer drop.

Although it's fantastic to see these incredible birds nesting in our towns and cities, sleek modern architecture can pose a problem. Fledging is a precarious time for peregrines in particular as it takes a couple of days for them to learn how to manoeuvre their wings and tail and use the wind to their advantage. And while adult peregrine falcons are amazing aerial predators, it takes juveniles a little time to become such masters of the air.

Usually, young peregrines will make a very short maiden flight, maybe of less than a hundred metres, before turning round to return to the nest or a nearby perch. Natural nest sites are more likely to have nooks and crannies to cling on to if the chicks make an error of judgement. If a fledging peregrine loses height in an urban area, it can be faced with the sheer walls of an office block and, with nowhere to land, it may end up falling to the ground.

The peregrine family that *Springwatch* followed in Bath during 2012 has had quite a few fledglings jumping the nest too early over the years. One ended up grounded on the local cricket pitch and another fell down a chimney (fortunately, into the house of the president of the local RSPB!). The male chick of 2012 nearly had a watery ending – he was mobbed by gulls soon after fledging and had to be recovered from the River Avon before being safely returned to a nearby roof. If these fledglings hadn't been rescued they almost certainly would have perished. Many juvenile peregrines aren't as lucky, with perhaps only a quarter to a third of fledglings making it to adulthood.

High Flyers

I love watching swifts and house martins catching insects, but what exactly are all the insects doing so high up in the air? I have seen low-flying swifts but mostly they seem to feed high up, above tree level. *Karen*

When they have hungry chicks to feed, a swift can collect up to 10,000 insects a day. To find that much food every day, there must be a huge number of flies, mosquitoes and other small animals up in the air. The swifts and martins might appear to be darting through a clear blue sky but actually there are millions, if not billions, of tiny creatures floating around up there. The air is full of so-called 'aerial plankton' – just like plankton in the sea this is made up of a huge variety of life forms, from minuscule bacteria to large insects such as moths.

Why are they all up there? Well, some flying insects will just be going about their daily business, looking for nectar, prey or other food sources. Others may get swept up into the atmosphere, especially later in the day as the air warms up and thermals form. Swifts, house martins and other predators will follow, sometimes hundreds of metres upwards. Many small insects and bugs will disperse short distances on the wind in search of a new place to live or a mate, simply standing up on their back legs and catching a ride on a gust of wind. Some moths and butterflies travel more purposefully, migrating hundreds of kilometres with the aid of high-altitude air currents.

Many species of spider also quite deliberately use the wind to move around. They find a suitable high spot such as a fence or hedgerow, point their abdomen skywards and eject fine threads of silk into the air. A breeze will catch the threads and carry these 'ballooning' spiders upwards. Much like a hot-air balloon, the spider is at the mercy of the prevailing air currents but on a good wind can travel several kilometres to a new home.

The sky is a veritable highway, full of small invertebrates travelling from one place to another. Planes have been used to sample the air at altitude and many insects have been found several kilometres up, but the world record goes to a termite caught at 5,800 metres, nearly as high as the summit of Mount Kilimanjaro! It's not just the altitude that's impressive; the sheer numbers of insects up there are mind-boggling too. Recent research used radar to detect airborne invertebrates and estimated that during an average summer month, three billion insects, from moths to tiny aphids, would pass through a square kilometre column of air over the southern English countryside. That's equivalent to one metric ton of insects passing overhead each month. No wonder the swifts and martins are busy!

A Swift Snooze

During the spring and summer months we get a lot of swifts screaming overhead as they chase each other, flying up under the eaves of nearby houses and generally feeding on flies and insects. We see them right through until 8pm, then they seem to get higher and higher until they are no longer visible. Does this mean they go up to a very high altitude to sleep on the wing or do they simply move off to another area to continue feeding through the night? *Dean*

Swifts have always been mysterious birds and there is still much to learn about them. Their lifestyle is so enigmatic because most of it is spent in the air, making these birds difficult to study. About 80,000 pairs of swifts arrive from Africa every summer for a brief three-month breeding period. They can live for more than 20 years and may fly 4.5 million kilometres in that time – equivalent to flying to the moon and back six times. Swifts eat, mate and sleep on the wing and, unless they're injured, they only land to lay their eggs. It's staggering to think that a young swift will spend its first two or three years entirely airborne until it is ready to breed.

Swifts spend the night on the wing and, as Dean observed, they fly up to high altitudes each night. Swedish scientists have studied these nocturnal flights using radar and found that swifts reach up to 3,000 metres, the same height at which light aircraft fly, where there is less turbulence and few, if any, predators. Swifts orientate into the wind, allowing them to glide rather than flap their wings, thus maximising their energy efficiency. During the night they weave slowly from side to side to avoid drifting too far away from their home area.

It's unlikely that swifts 'sleep' as we experience it; instead they shut down half of their brain at a time. Like us, birds have two types of sleep: a deep, slow-wave sleep (SWS) and rapid eye-movement (REM) sleep, during which we may experience dreams. SWS can occur in one or both hemispheres of the brain while REM only occurs in both at once. By falling into a slow-wave sleep on one side of the brain, a swift could keep one eye open and navigate while asleep. Swifts probably don't use REM sleep at all as they would have to shut down both sides of the brain at once to do so, which would cause their muscles to relax and would lead to unfortunate gravity-induced consequences!

Far From Home?

When I was planting some bedding plants I found two small frogs in my border; in fact, I almost skewered one with my gardening fork. Why would they be there when I am not near any water? *Jan*

It's actually a bit of a myth that adult frogs live in ponds all the time. Like most amphibians, they spend part of their life in water and part on land. In fact, this is the origin of the word amphibian, from the Greek *amphi* meaning 'of both kinds' or 'double', and *bios* meaning 'life', referring to the dual aquatic and terrestrial lifestyles of frogs, toads and newts. A frog's eggs and young will only survive in water, but once tadpoles have metamorphosed into froglets they are not so reliant on ponds.

Adults may move into gardens or grassland and are often found up to 500 metres from the nearest water. Frogs will be happy in any damp spot with a supply of food such as insects, slugs and worms, so a patch of long grass or a well-watered flower border would be ideal. They just need somewhere with enough humidity to keep their skin moist. Although adult frogs have lungs, much of their respiration occurs via their clammy, highly permeable skin. Oxygen diffuses through mucus and membrane into the capillaries. Carbon dioxide diffuses in the opposite direction. Frogs can also absorb water through their skin and in the heat of the day frogs will seek out damp places. They often take refuge under rocks or mulch in a flowerbed, out of the way of predators. In summer, they may only be active in the cool of the night. Frogs are often difficult to spot as their brown/green skin makes excellent camouflage and they may sit motionless for long periods of time. If threatened, they will use their powerful long legs to leap away from danger. Frogs are mainly solitary so it's unusual to find two together.

Frogs need only return to a pond when they're ready to breed, at about three years old. They usually find their way back to the pond where they were born. Until then, welcome them as guardians of your bedding plants because a large part of their diet can be made up of slugs and snails.

Ant-Astic

Every year, on very hot days, we always have flying ants erupt from under the grass. They fly away, never to be seen again. Why does this happen only on warm days and where do they go? *Polite Ringo Rabbit*

What you're seeing is the mating frenzy of the black garden ant, *Lasius niger*. For most of the year, any ants you'll see will be sterile, female workers, but in summer the colony produces male drones and immature queens. When conditions are right, swarms of these males and unfertilised queens (also known as princesses) take to the air in search of mates. As their name might suggest, the princesses are demanding lovers, often trying to out-fly the males so that only the strongest suitors will be successful. Each queen usually mates with several males during this 'nuptial' flight, acquiring enough sperm to fertilise the millions of eggs she will produce in her lifetime.

What triggers a 'flying ant day'? Well, ants in the same area tend to emerge within a day or so of each other, reducing the chances of being caught by a predator and maximising the opportunity of finding a mate from another colony. How this emergence is synchronised is something of a mystery but it is thought to be related to weather. Ants can sense temperature, humidity and day length and choose to emerge during warm, humid conditions – often a hot day preceded by wet weather. Rain or wind would hamper their flight and humidity means the soil is nice and soft, making it easier for the queen to burrow and make a nest. The notion of a single, annual flying ant day is something of a myth. The date varies across the country and there are simply peaks of activity when the weather is right.

After mating, the male's sole purpose in life has been accomplished and he will die soon afterwards. If the queen manages to dodge birds and other predators making the most of the flying ant feast, she starts a new colony. She sheds her wings, as they are no longer needed, and digs a chamber underground to raise the first of her larvae. The queen then effectively becomes an egg-laying machine for the colony and may live for up to 15 years.

A Prickly Problem

My nine-year-old daughter, Cerys, has three questions about hedgehogs: Are baby hedgehogs born with prickles? Do hedgehogs ever lose their prickles? Do old hedgehogs' prickles turn grey? Many thanks. *Pal Natter*

Well, the first question is enough to make anyone wince! Baby hedgehogs are born with prickles but, thankfully for the mother, they remain under the skin until a few hours after birth. Each tiny pink hoglet emerges with what appear to be pimples covering their skin, and small, white spines poke through shortly afterwards. After 36 hours a second set of brown spines starts to grow and will cover the baby by the time it is a couple of weeks old. Hoglets leave the nest at about six weeks of age and will then gradually grow their adult set of spines.

Hedgehog spines form a remarkable defence system. An adult hedgehog has between 5,000 and 7,000 spines, each of which are 2–3 centimetres long and brown at the base with a creamy-coloured tip. These spines are modified hollow hairs, toughened with keratin, which grow from follicles in the skin, and each one is attached to a tiny muscle so that it can be moved independently. They cover every part of the hedgehog's body apart from the face, legs and underparts. The spines protect them from predators and act as a shock absorber if they fall. If threatened, the hedgehog will curl up and erect all its spines, drawing in its feet and head to become an impenetrable spiky ball. Few predators would even tackle this and only badgers are known to successfully make it past the prickles.

Hedgehogs do lose their spines, but not all at once, because they are so vital for protection. The spines are moulted individually, with each one lasting about 18 months before it is replaced. Occasionally, hedgehogs will lose their spines due to injuries or illness, but usually they will grow back, though this may take a while.

Do old hedgehogs go grey? Apparently, spines may become a bit lighter with age, but there is so much colour variation across the population, including some hedgehogs with a few white spines, some completely blonde individuals as well as true albinos, that it would be impossible to say a 'grey' hedgehog is an older one.

The Early Bird

How do blackbirds detect where worms or invertebrates are located in the soil? Is it by sound, touch or sight? After spells of heavy rain my garden is now soft enough for the blackbirds to scavenge, so how do they do it? Any ideas? *Jack*

Blackbirds used to be woodland birds but as forest cover decreased they moved into our parks and gardens. Blackbirds have become one of our most common garden birds, with nearly 5 million breeding pairs resident in the

UK. Blackbirds are more productive in gardens than in woodland because their nests are predated less often and because in this situation they also live longer.

You might think that you've got just one pair of blackbirds that come and go in your garden, but chances are it's actually twenty or thirty different birds. It's not uncommon to find a hundred different blackbirds living per square kilometre in suburban areas. Gardens make perfect hunting grounds for blackbirds because they offer muddy ditches, wet areas under bushes and stretches of grassland for them to forage in.

Blackbirds probably employ a combination of senses when hunting, using sight, sound and touch to track down a worm. A blackbird runs across a patch of lawn, stopping and starting, cocking its head to one side, looking and listening for prey. Their eyes are on the side of their head, giving them excellent peripheral vision, while moving the head around helps their ears pin down the exact position of any rustling prey.

Blackbirds often root around in leaf litter looking for small invertebrates and worms, as well as pecking around in the soil. The beak is quite sensitive, and so by probing it in the ground the blackbird may detect any moving prey. Experience is important too and blackbirds get better at discovering food with age. One study found that two-year-old birds were twice as successful at finding large prey as one-year-olds.

Earthworms are a particularly important part of the blackbird's diet. Watch them closely and you may see blackbirds stamping their feet, using the vibration to attract worms to the surface. On feeling the vibration, earthworms may head upwards, perhaps because it sounds like falling rain or because it resembles the movements of hunting moles. Either way, the method often works and the stamping blackbird is rewarded with a juicy meal.

Second Home

On 10 July I noticed a squirrel going into a recently used magpie nest. The squirrel started refurbishing the nest with leaves. Is this usual? *Polly*

Polly doesn't mention whether this was a red or grey squirrel but both build nests known as dreys. These provide a safe place to give birth, to rest during the day and to sleep at night. These nests are about the size of a football, constructed from twigs and leaves then lined with soft moss, lichen and more leaves. Dreys are usually tucked into a fork against the trunk and supported by a branch, though squirrels may also use large holes in trees as drey sites. Winter dreys tend to be whole spheres with cosy interiors, whereas summer ones might be just a shallow platform.

Each squirrel may use several dreys and some individuals have been known to use as many as eight, although the average is three. Several squirrels may share a drey, or use the same one on different days.

It's quite easy to confuse a large bird's nest with a drey, especially from the ground. One clue is that squirrels tend to break off living twigs from trees with the leaves still attached, while birds collect dead, bare twigs. However, Polly knows that particular nest had been occupied by a magpie family so it seems the squirrel may simply have been renovating it. Both red and grey squirrels are resourceful creatures and will take over or adapt abandoned birds' nests. Grey squirrels have been observed using old rook nests, and a magpie's would be just the right size too.

Landlubber Gulls

I've always wondered, why have we got seagulls flying around Dartmoor when the nearest seashore is 40 kilometres away? *Beverley*

Firstly, to be pedantic, there's no such thing as 'seagulls' – there are in fact about 24 different species of gull seen regularly in the UK. Until recently they were mostly associated with the coast. However, herring gulls, black-backed gulls and even kittiwakes often move inland, to feed or roost. They are very adaptable birds and over the past fifty years or so our growing levels of waste have provided plenty of new feeding opportunities for them.

In 1956 Parliament passed the Clean Air Act, which prevented the burning of rubbish and meant that increasing amounts of our refuse went to landfill sites. Gulls soon took advantage of our leftovers and some began to settle inland. They aren't settling inland just because of the plentiful food – our rooftops provide secure, undisturbed nest sites away from predators. Street lighting also allows the gulls to forage late into the night. Cities are also a few degrees warmer than the surrounding countryside, which enables the gulls to breed earlier in the year. All these factors mean that more and more gulls of various species are breeding in our towns and cities – it's estimated that 100,000 pairs nest in urban areas.

Urban herring gulls are certainly faring much better than their rural and coastal cousins, which are rapidly declining in number – the population as a whole has halved over the past few decades. No one is sure why coastal herring gulls are becoming more scarce, but perhaps it is because less prey is available to them. Changes in commercial fishing practices in recent years mean that less bycatch is thrown overboard now, so gulls may no longer benefit from this free handout. Whatever the cause, rural gulls may soon be outnumbered by urban ones.

It's impossible to tell whether the gulls that Beverley saw on Dartmoor were urban or coastal birds because herring gulls will travel up to 50 kilometres or more to find food. Although there may be no landfill sites in the middle of Dartmoor, gulls can often be seen following a tractor, picking over the newly-ploughed soil, or looking for small prey in the fields. If it was late afternoon, the gulls may have been heading to bed. Several gull species fly inland to roost overnight, sometimes in their thousands, on sheltered reservoirs, gravel pits and lakes. Whether they were looking for food or shelter, any city dweller who has been kept awake by these raucous birds knows that gulls are certainly not restricted to the seaside!

Grounded

Why do some birds, such as warblers, nest on the ground? Surely it would be safer for them to nest in the trees, avoiding foxes, etc.? *Charlotte*

Predators present a huge challenge to any bird trying to bring up a family, but one would assume that ground-nesting species would be particularly vulnerable. Nevertheless, a huge variety of birds do nest on the ground, from small songbirds such as skylarks to gamebirds like grouse, waders such as curlew and lapwings, to large birds of prey including hen harriers. Why? Well, often the habitats they live in, such as open moorland or grassland, don't have any trees so there is simply no choice left to them but to nest on the ground.

To overcome this, these birds and their nests have been honed through evolution to be as inconspicuous to predators as possible. Some nests may be hidden in long grass or heather but others are out in the open, perhaps just a small scrape in the soil or gravel. Eggs and chicks are usually highly camouflaged and often the adult bird is cryptic too. In species such as woodcock, the parent will sit stock still until a predator is right upon it.

Others have very secretive behaviour. For example, skylark parents land a short distance away from their nest and scurry through the grass to it, a tactic intended to deter predators from finding its location. Islands without terrestrial predators such as foxes and hedgehogs can also be a safe haven for ground-nesting birds.

On the face of it, nesting on the ground seems a very risky strategy but many birds do successfully raise families this way. We can give them a helping hand by treading carefully when walking in areas where they may nest and by keeping dogs on a lead during the breeding season.

Woodworking Wasps

Why are wasps so attracted to our wooden garden bench? They settle down almost as if they were drinking from it. When they fly off they leave a little wet patch behind, but once that dries, there's no visible sign they've been there. *Jane*

The wasps drawn to Jane's bench were looking for building material; and if she looked very closely she may notice narrow white lines where the wasps have used their powerful jaws to rasp off tiny bits of wood. The wet patch she describes will be their saliva. The wasps don't eat the wood but use it to construct their incredibly complex nests. They mix the chewed wood with their saliva to create a papery paste, which is then laid down to form the walls and internal structure. The nest has a central column with layers of flat combs where the larvae develop within individual hexagonal cells. The whole structure is encased in thin, papery outer walls. It's quite a feat of engineering and has inspired some people to change their opinion of wasps:

Recently we have had wasps come to one particular fence post in our garden to strip the wood. It's fascinating. Sometimes there are three workers on the same post at a time! The nibbling noises are so loud we thought at first it was a mouse trapped in our shed. They come every day now. I've never been a big fan of wasps, but I have a new respect for them now. They deserve as much interest and praise as other creatures receive. Grace

It's strange how people have such opposing attitudes to wasps and bees. Bees are generally held in affection while wasps are vilified. Wasps really are amazing insects, though, and don't deserve their fearsome reputation. One fisherman agrees and has developed such a fondness for wasps that he allows them to feed from his hands:

I work outdoors handling fish all day. Throughout the summer wasps come down to the buckets of dead fish and chew small balls of fish meat off to take back to the nest. Very often they land on my hands which are covered in fish oil and try to chew 'fish' off my hands. It is fascinating to watch, and whereas before I was nervous of wasps, I now love them! In ten years of watching this behaviour I have only been stung twice and both times the fault was mine – I didn't see the wasp and accidentally squeezed it. Lesley G

Wasps rarely sting humans if left unharrassed and their predatory habits make them a gardener's friend. There are hundreds of species of wasp in the UK and most of them are carnivorous, helping to keep pests such as caterpillars and aphids under control. If they're treated with respect, watching them can provide as much enjoyment and awe as birdwatching.

Taking a Toll

My dad followed a barn owl across the Severn Bridge yesterday. It was following the road directly. Do barn owls use roads to navigate like pigeons do? *Fran*

There have been quite a few studies on homing pigeons describing how they use roads when navigating back to their roost, sometimes following their path so closely that they turn off at certain junctions and even take particular exits on roundabouts. This may not be the most direct route 'as the crow flies', and shows that pigeons are using the roads as landmarks to find their way around.

Barn owls probably don't need to navigate like this though, as they tend to travel only short distances. They usually hunt within a couple of kilometres of their roost or nest. Even juveniles leaving home to find their own territory don't travel much more than 12 kilometres or so. Unfortunately, meandering around the countryside looking for a new home is very dangerous because major roads represent a deadly hazard for barn owls. The Barn Owl Trust estimates that Britain's barn owls produce roughly 12,000 young each year and of these 3,000 may be killed on roads. In 2012, 27 per cent of barn owl deaths reported to the British Trust for Ornithology were attributed to collisions with vehicles. The dangers of fast-moving traffic have become such a problem that most major roads have no barn owls living within 500 metres either side.

What's behind this grim statistic? Well, barn owls tend to fly slowly and quite low, at about 3 metres or less above the ground, so they are in the path of moving vehicles. Minor roads don't seem to be anywhere near as deadly, perhaps because traffic is slower and they often have hedgerows or trees that encourage barn owls to fly across the road above the height of vehicles. What can we do? One suggestion is that major roads should be planted with high hedges or trees each side to push barn owls up to a safer height when crossing.

Motorways and fast traffic can't be eliminated but we can help barn owls in other ways. There may be a lack of suitable nest sites in your area, so if you live well away from busy roads consider putting up an artificial nest box. Barn owls also need rough grassland where they can hunt for voles and mice. If you manage farmland or pasture, try leaving areas where the grass can grow up to provide cover for small mammals. With luck, you may be rewarded with the glorious sight of a barn owl gliding silently across the fields as it looks for prey.

Quite a Mouthful

My six-year-old son Reggie, who went with us to Skomer Island last week, wants to know what is the biggest number of fish that a puffin can get in its beak? *Nessie*

How do puffins manage to catch multiple sand eels?
Wolfman Matt

Puffins spend most of their lives out at sea but each April about 6,000 pairs return to breed on the island of Skomer off the coast of Pembrokeshire. They nest in burrows, often old rabbit warrens, each pair raising a single chick. The parents hunt offshore for small fish, mainly oily, nutritious sand eels, and each puffin can bring back dozens at a time, all neatly lined up in their brightly coloured beaks. According to the British Trust for Ornithology, the largest number of sand eels ever recorded being carried in a puffin's beak is 83! Those fish must have been pretty small, though, as the one thing that strikes most people when they see a puffin for the first time is their size – they're much smaller than you might expect, roughly 30 centimetres from beak to tail.

When most seabirds catch food for their chicks, they swallow the prey and then regurgitate it back at the nest. Puffins are different, though; they can catch dozens of fish and transport them in their beak back to their chicks. This neat trick is due to their specialised beak; it doesn't open on a hinge like a blackbird or robin's bill; instead it has a special bone that allows the puffins to open their bill and keep both parts parallel. This means puffins can hold a row of fish without the ones at the tip of their beak falling out.

The beak also has serrated edges and backward-pointing spines on the palate and tongue that hold the fish in place. The puffin orientates each fish crosswise, with alternating heads and tails hanging out at the sides. They carry on diving and adding fish until their beak is full.

Puffins can dive for up to a minute at a time and reach depths of up to 70 metres. Incidentally, they are such good swimmers that people used to believe puffins were a cross between a bird and fish. This also meant that puffin meat was accepted by the Catholic Church as neither flesh nor fowl and could be eaten on Fridays and during Lent.

Both parents bring back food for the puffin chicks – delightfully named pufflings – which fledge in late summer. Once they have left the island, the juveniles remain at sea for several years until they return to find a mate and breed.

A Watery Demise

I saw a sparrowhawk in my garden take out a starling. It was struggling to kill it so it hopped across the lawn with its prey towards my pond. The sparrowhawk jumped in and, after flapping around a bit shocked, it appeared to be holding the starling under to drown it! I thought the sparrowhawk would become waterlogged after so long, so I went out to see if I could help (and to stop my Border Collie from trying to eat it!), but it flew up out of the water with ease. Is this normal behaviour for a sparrowhawk? *Sarah*

This is amazing behaviour to see and quite unusual. It's not unprecedented, though, and back in 2009 *Unsprung* showed footage of something similar, a sparrowhawk in Germany struggling with a magpie before dragging it off to a pond to drown it. It was quite gruesome to watch but it did appear that the sparrowhawk spotted the pond and took the magpie to it with the intention of killing it in the water.

This apparent planning or forethought is remarkable but sparrowhawks are very adept hunters. They use several strategies when hunting but generally rely on stealth and being able to sneak up on prey undetected. They are very agile in flight but can't sustain long chases – only one in ten attempted hunts will be successful. Sparrowhawks have long legs and claws that help them catch and handle prey. Once they have a bird on the ground, the sparrowhawk will stand on top of it and begin plucking, even if the prey is still alive.

If a large bird like a starling struggled for long the sparrowhawk could be injured, or at least become tired, so drowning would be a quick and effective way of overcoming the prey.

We received other sightings of the same behaviour:

With regard to the sparrowhawk drowning the magpie, I have also witnessed something similar. While visiting the cafe at Glenmore in the Cairngorms a couple of years ago I was enjoying watching the squirrels and birds feeding, when a sparrowhawk flew in and lifted a blackbird off one of the feeding tables. It then deliberately took the bird to a nearby shallow burn and held it under the water until it stopped flapping. It then flew off with the dead bird. I was told by the café staff that this was not the first such occurrence. Ronnie

We've seen this behaviour too. Right in the centre of Reading we saw a sparrowhawk drop down on a pigeon, struggle to fly away with it (the pigeon was roughly as big as the sparrowhawk), then deliberately dunk it into a nearby brook until it stopped moving, after which it flew away with its now non-struggling prey. Stephen

It seems that this method might be particularly useful when dealing with larger prey, such as pigeons and magpies. Male sparrowhawks are about half the size of females and rarely take prey larger than a blackbird, so it's likely to be females drowning the birds in these reports. Although this behaviour may seem macabre, sparrowhawks are simply highly efficient predators, and if you see them in your garden it's a sure sign that there is a healthy population of small birds in the area.

Going Underground

Do moles have eyes? *Chrissy*

How do moles meet? *Rob*

We have just been watching a mole running around in the garden. What was it doing above the ground? *Carol*

How do moles breathe underground? Is oxygen not at very low levels down there? *Wilt*

Moles are enigmatic creatures, spending their lives out of sight in the muddy gloominess of underground tunnels. Few of us ever have the luck to see a mole, just the molehills their digging leaves behind. This has led to many questions about their invisible lives – the ones above are just a selection.

Moles do have eyes but they are tiny, only about a millimetre across and well hidden in their dense, dark fur. Unsurprisingly for an animal that spends nearly all its life in darkness, their vision is limited. It's believed moles can differentiate between light and dark but not much more. This perfunctory eyesight would enable them to detect any holes in their tunnels and repair them. It also allows the tiny amount of light that makes it through the soil to control their body clocks, changing their behaviour with day length and determining when to mate during the spring.

Moles make up for their poor eyesight by using their other heightened senses. They have very sensitive whiskers and special sensory organs on their nose – these are called Eimer's organs after Theodor Eimer, the German zoologist who discovered them in 1871. The skin has bulbous papillae (tiny bulges about a tenth of a millimetre in diameter) that are stuffed full of nerve endings. These can detect any movement in the soil and help the mole to build up a three-dimensional picture of its world. Some North American moles have also been shown to smell in stereo. Just as we can hear in stereo and determine which direction a sound is coming from, these moles can use their nostrils to tell where the source of smell can be found. They literally follow their noses to find a juicy worm or sniff out another mole. Moles find food by patrolling their tunnels and eating any worms, beetle larvae or other grubs that have fallen in. If they find a surplus of worms, they bite them and store them for another meal. The worms remain alive but are paralysed by a toxin in the mole's saliva.

As a rule, moles don't meet. They are solitary creatures and fiercely defend their territory. One exception is in early spring when males head off to find a mate. Generally, they stay underground, digging new tunnels and extending their territory on the hunt for females. When the male finds a female, he may be met with aggression, and after mating the pair go their separate ways again. The other exception is that occasionally some tunnels are used by several moles in adjoining territories but individuals may still avoid each other by using the tunnel at different times of day.

Any mole you find above ground is probably a youngster that has mistakenly broken through the surface while trying to find or create its own territory. Moles may also emerge to collect nesting material such as dry grass. Either way, they are in great danger and often fall victim to owls.

Mole tunnels have no entrance or exit holes so there is little or no fresh air flowing through them. This affects the composition of the air in mole tunnels. Above ground, the atmosphere is composed of 21 per cent oxygen and only a tiny 0.03 per cent of it is carbon dioxide. The mole's vigorous digging uses up oxygen and produces carbon dioxide to such an extent that the air in mole tunnels may be just 14.3 per cent oxygen and a whopping 5.5 per cent carbon dioxide. That level of carbon dioxide alone would make us feel very unwell, but combined with a lack of oxygen it could prove fatal. So how do moles survive? They have what's known as a high blood oxygen affinity; that is, their blood is much more efficient at absorbing oxygen than that of other mammals of a similar size. They are perfectly adapted to their subterranean lives.

Tripping the Light Fantastic

If moths are attracted to light why don't they just come out in the daytime? *Mark*

How do moths find their way in the dark? *Matt*

Why are moths fascinated by artificial lighting? *Sophie*

Firstly, not all moths are nocturnal; there are some particularly beautiful ones that fly during the day, such as the cinnabar and burnet moths with scarlet and black wings. Most species are more cryptic, with wings in shades of grey and brown that melt into the background when they are resting during the day. It's thought that moths evolved to be nocturnal to avoid daytime predators such as birds. However, the evolutionary arms race continues at night with bats, who are also partial to a juicy mouthful of moth.

To find its way around in the dark, an animal must be able to detect its immediate surroundings and navigate around them. Unlike bats, moths can see and have excellent nocturnal vision. They have compound eyes that give them a wide field of vision so they can see behind their heads and spot any threats, but this is at the expense of the sharpness of the image. Humans have what's known as a 'constant visual stream', with a new image constantly replacing the previous one, but moths use 'neural summation', which means they store images over time. This allows them to build up a picture in lower light conditions, but this also leads to a blurry image. Moths can also see ultraviolet light which many flowers reflect, perhaps making it easier to pinpoint them in the dark. Hawkmoths can even differentiate between colours in the near darkness of starlight, whereas we would be colour-blind. Moths also use smell to locate flowers and track down the pheromones of other moths, though the pheromones glow very faintly too.

So they can see, but how do they navigate? This is still something of a mystery. Some entomologists think moths, especially migratory species, use the position of the moon to guide them. The moon is so distant that it is a relatively fixed reference point in the sky and if moths fly at a particular angle to it they can navigate – it's a behaviour called transverse orientation.

This may also explain the 'moth to a flame' phenomenon, when moths fly towards artificial lights and candles in an occasionally fatal attraction. It seems that moths become disorientated, mistaking the light for the moon, but, unlike the moon, its position relative to the moth will move as the moth flies. For example, if we walk down a street at night the moon stays in the same position in the sky but the street lamps pass by as we progress. If we were using the moon for navigation, we could set a course – for example, by keeping it on our right. If we were confused by a street lamp we'd end up going round in circles whenever we came across one. The same may be true for moths. If a moth attempts to maintain its course by keeping a constant angle relative to the moon, it will adjust its flight and can end up spiralling towards the light source. Another theory is that the light dazzles the moth's compound eyes and so it is drawn towards it.

Whatever the mechanism, this attraction makes it easier for us to get a closer look at these fascinating insects. You can make a simple moth trap by hanging up a white sheet and shining a light on it. They might be tricky to identify (there are more than 2,500 species of moth in the UK compared to about 60 species of butterfly), but admiring the sheer variety and subtle beauty of moths will show that they deserve just as much affection and attention as their blousier cousins, the butterflies.

Soggy Bees

After the downpour at the weekend I noticed there were quite a lot of bees on the flowers in my garden. Some were dead and others seemed to be very sleepy! Is there anything I can do to help them? *Trish*

Bees really suffer in cold or wet weather and our recent inclement summers have badly affected bee populations. There are about 260 species of bee in the UK and they need warm conditions to forage. Flowers produce less nectar and pollen in cold, damp weather and rain deters bees from flying. This is not just bad for bees – farmers can suffer too because bees and other flying insects are important pollinators. Insects are estimated to contribute over £400 million each year to the UK economy by pollinating crops such as peas, apples, tomatoes and soft fruit. During sustained wet weather, beekeepers may resort to feeding their bees with sugar syrup to prevent starvation as the honey bees can't produce enough honey to feed themselves, let alone enough to harvest. Wild bees don't have this luxury.

Honeybees tend to stay in the hive if the weather is wet, but bumblebees are larger and can tolerate cooler temperatures and light rain. If they get caught out in a shower the cold, wet conditions lower their metabolism and make them appear sleepy. If they become sodden, they may not be able to generate enough metabolic heat to fly. This can be fatal and makes them an easy target for predators too.

What can you do if you find soggy bees? They will often crawl onto a sheet of kitchen towel if you offer it to them, enabling you to move them gently out of the rain onto a sheltered flower where they may be able to find some nectar. Handle them with care, though – bees' wings are fragile and bumblebees can sting if they feel threatened. If they're really struggling you can help them to dry out by putting them in a warm place on some kitchen towel. If the bee still looks a bit dozy, try offering some clean sugar solution which you can make by dissolving plain sugar in a bit of warm water. Pour a little into a very shallow dish or bottle top, or soak another piece of kitchen towel. Don't use honey as it may contain viruses or diseases to which the bee has no immunity. Once the bee has warmed up, dried off and recovered, release it somewhere dry as soon as possible.

These measures might help in the short term, but if you really want to do your bees a favour, plant varieties of flowers that bloom throughout the year, from spring until late summer, and will provide plenty of nectar and pollen. Many seed packets and plant labels now have symbols showing if a particular plant is bee-friendly. If you don't have a garden, even a window box or hanging basket will help.

Well Spotted

My nine-year-old daughter would love to ask a question: 'why do ladybirds have spots and why do some have more than others?' *Evie*

An old wives' tale says that a ladybird's age can be told from the number of spots on its back – a lovely thought but untrue! Some ladybirds have more spots than others simply because they are different species; there are two-spot, five-spot, seven-spot and other varieties all the way up to twenty-four-spot ladybirds. Most ladybirds won't live for much longer than a year, though, so the old wives' tale is way off the mark.

There are 46 species of ladybird in the UK, but only 26 actually resemble a 'traditional' ladybird. We think of ladybirds as having scarlet wingcases (called elytra) and black spots, but there are all sorts of other colour variations: black with red spots, yellow, orange and black forms. Some have no spots while others have stripes. These bright colours and striking patterns are a warning signal to any potential predators such as birds. It's a phenomenon called 'aposematism' in which animals advertise that they taste unpleasant or are poisonous. If threatened, ladybirds can release a sticky, yellow substance from their joints called 'reflex blood'. This smells foul and contains toxic, bitter-tasting chemicals called alkaloids which deter most animals from eating them. In theory, any predator that tastes the reflex blood will associate that unpleasant experience with the ladybird's distinctive patterns and learn to avoid them in future.

This apparent immunity from being eaten has given the ladybird a sacred reputation. Their name comes from 'Our Lady's Bird' – Our Lady referring to the Virgin Mary, and the symbolism of the seven-spot ladybird. In early paintings, the Virgin Mary is depicted wearing red robes (blue came much later) and the seven spots represent her seven joys and seven sorrows. Of course, ladybirds are beetles, but when the name arose, any flying animal was known as a 'bird' just as any aquatic creature was called a fish. There are religious connotations in other languages too; for example, in German they are called *Marienkäfer*, which translates as Mary's beetle. Many different cultures believe that ladybirds bring good luck and they're certainly welcomed by gardeners. Most species are carnivorous and their aphid-eating abilities are legendary.

What a Wag

Why do wagtails wag their tails? Is it to help them balance, impress a mate, or does nobody know? *Nature Lover*

This is another biological conundrum – no one really knows why they wag their tails (if only we could ask them!) but there are several theories. The three species of wagtail that breed in the UK – the pied, yellow and grey – all wag their tails to some degree. They all catch their prey in a similar way, too, which has led some people to think that tail wagging may be important when they're foraging.

Wagtails are insectivores and feed on the ground, often near water, hunting for insects, beetles and spiders. They often flush small insects into the air, so perhaps this is aided by their jerky movements and tail wagging. Wagtails also 'flycatch', flying from a perch to hover and weave through the air snatching at flying insects. Their long tail may help them manoeuvre, acting like a rudder as they dart about.

Another theory is that tail wagging is a form of communication that shows dominance or submission within a flock. Pied wagtails in particular will gather to roost in their hundreds, so there may be some credence to this, but wagtails wag pretty much constantly, even when alone. A recent study also suggested that tail wagging may be a way of showing any potential predators that the wagtail is alert and vigilant to any attack, as if saying, 'I've got my eyes peeled, so don't even bother'.

Of course, none or all of these theories may be correct. Tails have many uses and there's no reason why a wagtail couldn't multi-task!

Hello Caller

Do starlings make weird telephone noises? We have one that is nesting in our eaves and makes these noises from morning until night! It quite often makes us jump for the telephone. *P.*

Starlings are well-known mimics. For centuries, starlings have been kept in captivity and taught to speak. Nearly 2,000 years ago, Pliny the Elder wrote about the starling's ability to learn human words. Mozart kept a pet starling for three years and formed a kind of symbiotic relationship with it. He wrote some of its phrases into his music and the bird would sing snippets of concertos back to him. Mozart loved the starling so much that when it died he held an elaborate funeral for it, complete with priests and a poem he'd written in its honour.

Starlings adopt the sounds that they hear around them into their calls, whether that's human speech when kept in captivity or the cacophony of a city. They will reproduce man-made sounds, like a ringing phone, as well as copy natural ones such as the calls of tawny owls, curlews and other birds. They've been known to mimic car alarms and chainsaws, and during the Second World War they even duplicated the ominous whine of an approaching doodlebug.

Starlings are very social birds and can gather in flocks of many thousands or even millions, so maybe it's not surprising that they have a wide variety of calls, from clicks and screeches to whistles and warbles. Some calls are made by the whole flock while other sounds are unique to the individual bird, allowing other starlings to recognise it. Sounds can be passed from one individual to another so that a bird making a particular sound may never have heard it first-hand. There are even local dialects in different regions.

Mimicked sounds make up only a small proportion of a starling's song, so why do they bother? By learning different sounds each starling can create a more elaborate song to impress potential mates – the song may not be particularly melodious but it is varied! Starlings continue to gather new sounds throughout their lives so older birds tend to have a wider repertoire than younger ones. Females seem to prefer more complex songs, perhaps because it indicates that the singer has more experience or longevity. Males with more complex songs also have more success in defending their territory and seeing off younger rivals. The bird singing in the Fords' eaves would probably have been a male protecting its nest.

Singing peaks during the breeding season but the song isn't just used to attract a mate or defend a nest. Males call throughout most of the year and females sing too, suggesting that singing also serves other functions within the flock. Next time you're close to a starling flock, listen carefully and see if you can pick out the calls of other birds or recognise any man-made sounds.

Eggstraordinary Treasure

Recently, I very mysteriously found a chicken egg in my flowerbed! Our garden backs onto a farmer's field and there is no access for members of the public without them coming through it or through our side gate. My husband assures me it was not a practical joke on his part! Any ideas? Yours curiously *Kate, Somerset*

Well, this is a mystery worthy of Hercule Poirot's little grey cells ... So let's start with a process of elimination. Could a chicken have laid the egg there? Kate doesn't mention if the neighbouring farmer keeps chickens, but even if they do it's unlikely to be from an escapee. Most domestic chickens have their wings clipped to stop them flying far, if at all. Could it be the egg of another species? Perhaps it was a mallard's egg – they often nest on the ground among vegetation and their eggs are about the same size as a hen's egg. Again, this is unlikely. Mallard eggs are generally a pale blue-green colour, though this does vary, and mallards usually have a large clutch. Twelve eggs or more is not uncommon so a single egg would be very unusual.

Assuming then that this is not a case of mistaken identity, which animal would put a chicken's egg in a flowerbed, and why? Kate doesn't mention if the egg was on top of the soil or buried in it. Either way, the most likely culprit is a fox. Foxes often store, or cache, food in a safe spot, and eggs are a particular favourite, often raided from a wild duck or goose nest. Eggs make a sizeable snack for a hungry fox and are ideal for storing. They are portable, easy to bury and not so smelly as to attract other scavengers. Hedgehogs and badgers don't cache food themselves but would happily raid a fox's larder. The soft soil of a flowerbed makes it a perfect place for a fox to bury its hoard, and eggs have even been discovered hidden in plant pots.

But where did the egg come from? If a fox had got into a hen house then it probably would have killed the chickens and cached some of those too. It may seem like wanton destruction when a fox kills a whole flock of hens but they're just making the most of a food bonanza, building up a store of surplus food for leaner times. Instead, it's likely that the egg was stolen from a compost heap or maybe someone nearby leaves food out for foxes. Perhaps the only way to discover the true identity of the mystery egg thief is to put the egg back where you found it and see if a fox returns to claim it.

Catching a Ride

Why do dolphins bow-ride? And won't they get hurt by the boats? We went to Wales a couple of years ago and my mum and dad took me out on a trip to see an island that was absolutely covered in gannets. On the way there, several dolphins came along for the ride and I was allowed to sit at the front of the dinghy to be near them. It truly was a wonderful experience but I was afraid they were going to get hit by the boat. *Charlie, aged 13*

It's magical when dolphins choose to join your boat, frolicking in front of the bow and allowing a brief but privileged window into their world. They often turn on their sides to look up through the water and get a better view of their spectators. Only those with a heart of stone could fail to be moved by the experience and many people describe feeling an awe-inspiring connection when it occurs. The reason behind this behaviour is open to interpretation though, and no one is really sure why dolphins do it.

Dolphins and porpoises have probably been swimming ahead of boats and ships since humans took to the water in vessels fast enough to create a bow wave. The ancient Greeks described the phenomenon in the Mediterranean and revered dolphins so highly that it was illegal to kill one. In essence, bow-riding dolphins are surfing, being pushed forwards and upwards by the pressure wave in the front of the boat. Dolphins are very good at it and often are completely propelled by the bow wave, not beating their tail at all. If you can see overboard you may see them jostling for position to gain the most momentum and you might be able to hear their clicks and squeaks as they communicate. They sometimes swim in the wake behind boats too. This behaviour is not unique to boats, though, as dolphins will ride ocean swells and breaking waves, and they have even been observed bow-riding ahead of large whales.

Why do they do it? Some biologists suggest that it's simply an efficient way of travelling from A to B. The dolphins get a power boost and use less energy by exploiting our sails or motors. This makes perfect sense, but dolphins have been known to head straight back to their original position after hitching a ride, which slightly scuppers the theory. Others think that the dolphins are purely having fun and may just enjoy the thrill of it. Dolphins are inquisitive, highly intelligent and very social animals, after all. This theory is controversial, though, because few non-human animals are believed to 'play', and much playful behaviour can be explained as animals learning and practising vital skills, such as hunting or fighting.

Whatever the reason, it's a joy to watch. And, don't worry, dolphins are masters of the sea and can outswim most boats. Bottlenose dolphins can cruise along at about 10 kilometres per hour but can reach up to 40 kilometres per hour in short sprints. They can easily peel off and head in another direction to avoid the bow when they've had enough. Fortunately, boats rarely hit bow-riding dolphins, though they can get entangled in fishing gear. As with most wildlife watching, it's never acceptable to chase after dolphins or encircle them. However, if dolphins do choose to bow-ride ahead of a boat, the skipper should maintain a steady speed and course, then enjoy the company!

Brazen Badgers

I'm interested in urban badgers, in particular about them having long-established territories which in some cases possibly go back to before urbanisation. We live in central Sheffield near 'Brocco Bank', which suggests a history of badgers in the area. It was built up in the nineteenth century. We hadn't been aware of badgers in the area until recently. At four o'clock in the morning a few weeks ago we were woken by some banging and scraping noises in our back garden, and by our two pet guinea pigs squeaking loudly. I ran downstairs and opened the back door to see a badger turn from the hutch and run away up the garden. It had broken in and killed both guinea pigs. This was obviously pretty shocking and upsetting, but also surprising as we never thought of badgers as hunters or likely to go to the trouble to break into a secure hutch. Have you ever heard of such a thing? *Will*

Will is right, badgers inherit setts from generation to generation and many may be several centuries old. Badger clans are very faithful to their setts and would not abandon them even when towns and cities like Sheffield were built around them. These days it is illegal to disturb an occupied badger sett and developers have to follow strict guidelines when building near them. In some places, badgers have adapted very well to living in an urban setting. A recent study in Brighton discovered a density of 30 badgers per square kilometre, higher than might be expected in the surrounding countryside, mainly due to the amount of food provided by badger-loving neighbours.

Although badgers are found across most of lowland Britain they tend to set up home in deciduous woodland which has grassland nearby that will provide plenty of their most important food, earthworms. A badger can eat over 200 earthworms on a good night, but they are omnivores and will eat a wide range of food including berries, fruit, cereals, insects and larger animals. In summer, birds and mammals can make up 20 per cent of their diet. They may not be the quickest predators but badgers will dig up young rabbits and raid the nests of rodents such as rats, voles and mice. Their strong claws can even make short work of hedgehogs.

Badgers are also opportunists. They have a very acute sense of smell and will regularly sniff out new food sources, especially during the summer when the soil may be too dry to dig for worms. They are big, robust animals, with males (boars) weighing up to 14 kilograms. They're strong too – large shoulder muscles make light work of digging, and badgers have been known to move a 25-kilogram boulder to get at food underneath. Their powerful jaws and claws can easily break into beehives to eat the honey and larvae, and, as Will unfortunately discovered, rabbit or guinea pig hutches are also vulnerable to attack. Badgers can easily climb over most fences and low walls so the best protection is to ensure your hutch or chicken coop is substantial. Loose chicken wire and thin or rotten wood won't deter a hungry badger (or fox, for that matter). Pens need to have sturdy walls, floors and roofs, and doors need to be latched securely each night. Attacks do tend to be more common in the summer months when other foods may be scarce, so take extra care then. With a few precautions the local badgers should leave your pets alone.

Summer Quiz

1. Foumart (pronounced 'foul-mart') is an old English name for which mammal?

    A. Fox
    B. Weasel
    C. Polecat
    D. Badger

2. What are these young animals called once they've grown up?

    A. Leveret
    B. Puffling
    C. Spat
    D. Squab

3. If you were walking on the beach and found a 'mermaid's purse', what might still be inside?

    A. Seaweed
    B. A baby shark
    C. A sea urchin
    D. Starfish

4. Which of these is *not* a species of moth?

    A. Garden tiger
    B. Feathered thorn
    C. Scarce footman
    D. Grizzled skipper

5. What is a baculum?

    A. An inner ear bone
    B. A tail feather
    C. A penis bone
    D. Part of an antler

6. How do glow-worms glow?

    A. A chemical reaction produces light.
    B. Shaking their tail rapidly creates enough friction to glow.
    C. They have light reflective scales that intensify moonlight.
    D. Phosphorescent cells absorb daylight and emit it at night.

Summer Quiz Answers

Question 1 Answer:

C. Polecat – named after their distinctive smell. 'Foumart' or 'foulmart' was also used as a term of abuse for a contemptible person.

Question 2 Answer:

A. Hare

B. Puffin

C. Oyster

D. Pigeon

Question 3 Answer:

B. A baby shark. A mermaid's purse is the egg case of sharks, skates and rays. They are often washed up onshore, usually after the fish has hatched out but sometimes with the embryo still inside.

Question 4 Answer:

D. The grizzled skipper is a butterfly seen in spring with a black-and-white chequerboard pattern on its wings. The rest are all moths.

Question 5 Answer:
C. A penis bone. Otters, rodents and many other male mammals have penis bones. Humans do not have bones in their penises but many other primates do, including gorillas and chimpanzees. The largest known baculum came from an extinct walrus discovered in 2007 and measuring 120 centimetres.

Question 6 Answer:
A. Glow-worms are flightless female beetles that emit a green light in their rear abdomen to attract males. The light is the product of a chemical reaction between oxygen and luciferin.

Autumn

Most of the year, frankly, brambles are nothing but a blasted nuisance, tearing at skin and clothes, sending out aggressive runners all over the garden – a prickly pest to be cut back whenever possible. But in autumn, I can forgive brambles practically anything, because now they produce blackberries. To bury your face in a bowl of freshly picked blackberries and inhale deeply is utterly intoxicating. Blackberry and apple pie, blackberry jam, blackberry jelly (if you can be bothered with muslin and upturned stools etc), are all heavenly. So, following my theme of 'iconic tastes and smells of the season', it's blackberries in autumn ... that and the smell of woodsmoke.

It's thought mankind first learnt how to control fire (rather than find it accidentally) somewhere around 250,000 years ago. Just think that your ancient ancestors – in skins, hunting mammoth, making flint tools just like Ray Mears (only a bit better) – would instantly recognise, and enjoy, the sweet scent of woodsmoke, just like you. It's a direct olfactory link with an unimaginably distant past. There's the aroma of chutney too, of course, filling the house with the eye-watering pungency of boiling vinegar as all the green tomatoes that never ripened get used at last – even though much of this will end up on the compost heap in six months' time. (Were you ever, really, going to eat 22 pots of the stuff?) Autumn is a time of unmistakeable scents.

Let's start inside the home then move outside to see what wildlife wonders autumn has to offer. As we head back indoors as the temperature begins to drop, so too do house spiders. You may not like this, but there's nothing we can do about it, it's cold out there! My favourite house spider (which can actually be found most of the year) is *Pholcus phalangioides* (a great Latin name on the tongue which means 'squint-eyed and finger like'), which is commonly called a 'daddy longlegs'. It has a tiny body and miles of skinny legs. Creep up on *Pholcus* and gently poke it as it hangs in the corner and you will see the most extraordinary thing. If threatened (by poking) this spider spins furiously around on a thread of silk. It spins so fast it literally becomes a blur, making it very difficult for a potential predator to know when or where to launch an attack. There are a variety of house spiders that come indoors in autumn and the most impressive of all is the huge (over 13 centimetres across) cardinal spider, so-called as one is supposed to have surprised Cardinal Wolsey by running across a tapestry, in flickering candlelight, when he was staying at Hampton Court. (How do these stories begin? Can that really be true?) In 2011 we ran an 'Unsprung' competition to find the biggest house spider in the UK, fully expecting people's claims not to be matched by actual measurement. We were wrong. The winner was 'Les4353' whose spider measured a whopping 14.2 centimetres across its legs. That's really quite big.

In the garden, look out for hornets. I always seem to see these magnificent yellow and chestnut-brown wasps late in the year. Yes, they are big and scary, but despite an intimidating appearance hornets are not aggressive and have to be really hassled before they sting. I used to live in an attic and during the winter, if I had the heating on, I would occasionally wake up to discover I was sharing my bed with dozy queen wasps whose hibernation had been disturbed by the heating. One memorable night I heard a deeper, much more serious buzzing on the duvet and, turning on the light, discovered a queen hornet beside me. I got her inside a cup and out of the window safely. Chris Packham had a number of hornets' nests actually in his bedroom as a youngster. He moved the nests into the room, if I recall correctly, in order to study them. There's nothing to say really, is there? Barking!

It's a good idea to leave some ivy in the garden when you're clearing up after the summer. In autumn this plant is an absolute godsend for wildlife trying to find food at the end of the year. It's worth going out and just listening to a patch of ivy in autumn, as it positively hums. There you can find late bees, wasps, butterflies and all sorts of other insects feeding on the nectar provided by inconspicuous ivy flowers, a final pit stop before winter. Some butterflies, especially brimstones, like to hibernate hidden away in a thick ivy patch.

Watch out for the strikingly colourful jays in gardens and parks. These pinky brown birds with their gorgeous turquoise wing flashes are actually a type of crow. The little azure-blue feathers making up the wing flashes have, occasionally, been made into scarves. It requires an awful lot of dead jays to make one scarf – a fact that caused the Duchess of Edinburgh to be shunned in Cannes in 1880 for wearing such a 'cruel' garment. Quite right too. Industrious jays collect acorns in autumn (they can carry up to eight at a time) and 'cache' them – a secret larder to uncover later in the winter. Individual jays can hide up to 5,000 acorns in autumn and research has shown they can then re-find an extraordinarily high percentage of them. Don't know about you, but I get lost hiding nine chocolate eggs around the garden for the children at Easter, so how a jay can find 5,000 is completely beyond my comprehension. Clever birds, these crows.

Let's move further afield to see two of the greatest spectacles of autumn. First, salmon. Salmon are born in freshwater but then spend many years out at sea. Eventually they have the remarkable ability to migrate back to the very same rivers in which they were born in order to reproduce themselves. I used to think they all came back in autumn; and while this is certainly true for some salmon, others come into freshwater much earlier in the year, as early as the spring. The fish that are fresh from the sea are dazzling, like a polished ingot of silver, whereas those that have been hanging around for a while 'put on the tartan', as they say on Scottish salmon rivers, going brown, green and red. Whatever time of year the salmon actually entered the river, in autumn they all move upstream, driven by some irresistible instinct to get to tiny shallow tributaries in order to mate and lay eggs. Salmon will try to get past any obstacle that gets in their way, even if it's a huge waterfall. It's quite a spectator sport to watch these mighty fish power themselves through the water, building up speed then leaping explosively into the air – as often as not falling back with a splash. When one finally makes it, a great cheer goes up from the watching crowd. Salmon can jump a staggering 12 feet vertically whilst leaping up waterfalls (this was actually measured at the Orrin falls in Ross-shire).

Finally, autumn is the time of the deer rut. Well, not for all deer; we have seven species of deer in the UK (some native and others introduced) but it is fallow and red deer that rut in autumn. We've covered rutting deer many times on *Autumnwatch* – the magnificent red deer on the island of Rum and the more delicate fallow deer in Petworth Park, in West Sussex – yet however many times you watch it, the rut is always thrilling, a sometimes shocking demonstration of explosive power. You don't have to go to the ends of the earth to see the rut, because these battles go on in parks up and down the country. In my younger days I was a very keen cross-country runner and my club used to train in Richmond Park, in London. To run through the park during the rut, in the dark, was seriously exciting. The bellowing and crashing, the clashing and snorting (often scarily close by) was quite something. Generally the stags completely ignore us puny humans, as they are only interested in one another, but please, keep your dog away from deer. I have seen some really idiotic people letting their pets approach the stags at this time of year, which can have dire consequences.

'Clinting' is my special word for autumn; 'clinting' is gathering up the shed antlers of deer, a pastime that is popular in parts of the USA where some people make quite a bit of money clinting.

Touchy Subject

Do birds' beaks have feeling? *Ampara*

A bird's beak or bill is a much more complex structure than it may at first appear. It's a multifunctional tool, used for delicate tasks such as preening feathers, building nests and turning eggs as well as handling food. Beaks come in a huge variety of shapes and sizes depending on a bird's diet. The broad, flat beaks of ducks and swans allow them to dabble underwater, goosanders' beaks have serrated edges to grip onto slippery fish, while birds of prey have razor-sharp hooks for tearing flesh apart. Birds can be amazingly dexterous with their beaks too, from prising open pine cones to cracking nuts and probing in mud. Some wading birds, such as snipe, have bendy beaks. The snipe can flex the upper beak upwards or downwards to pick up prey, a feat known as rhynchokinesis, from Greek and meaning 'moving snout'.

The bill has a bony framework covered by a layer of blood vessels and nerves which is encased in a thin, tough outer sheath made of keratin, the same material as our fingernails. Beaks continue to grow throughout a bird's life to counteract being worn down by constant use. Occasionally, *Springwatch* receives photos of birds such as blue tits with freakishly long beaks, where the rate of growth has far exceeded the rate at which a beak is worn down.

Waders such as curlew, knot and snipe have long, thin beaks that they use to probe into mud or wet sand to find their prey of worms and shellfish. Each wader species has a bill of a slightly different length so that they each forage at a particular depth in the mud. This means several species can feed on the same patch of estuary and avoid competition for food. But how do waders find their food when they can't see it hidden in the mud?

Some species of waterfowl and waders have particularly sensitive beaks and can hunt by touch alone. Many waders and ducks have a bill tip organ, a mass of touch-sensitive receptors called Herbst corpuscles and Grandry corpuscles that are arranged in rows on the inside rim of the upper and lower parts of the beak. The corpuscles detect movement and vibration. Touch-receptor cells are found throughout the beak but most are located at the tip. These cells enable ducks to sort through a beakful of gravel, weeds and other matter to reject the inedible parts of food, just as we might use our fingertips to feel around in a lucky dip bran tub at a fete. The bill tip organ also allows waders probing in mud to detect any movements made by their prey, such as wriggling ragworms or small shellfish.

One species of knot has been shown to use an even more sophisticated method of finding food. When they probe in wet sand or mud a pressure wave radiates out through the water and the birds can detect anything that lies in its path, in a very similar way to how sonar works. By repeatedly probing in one area the knot can perceive the currents and pressures created around objects and effectively 'see' in the mud to detect its prey. So, yes, many birds' beaks have a very acute sense of touch.

Ice, Ice Baby

Why are baby grey seals born white? And how does a mother recognise her pup from others? *James*

In the UK, the grey seal's breeding season progresses clockwise around the coast from the southwest. The first pups are born in the Scilly Isles and Cornwall in August or September, then births around the Scottish coast occur during October or November and the final pups are born in Norfolk in January. Most animals' young have some form of camouflage but grey seal pups are born with a creamy white fur called lanugo that stands out like a beacon on rocky beaches or grassy islands where they breed. This white fur is probably a relic left over from when Britain experienced an ice age thousands of years ago. In other parts of the grey seal's range, including the Baltic and northern Canada, mothers give birth in snowy or icy landscapes where the lanugo coat is less conspicuous and a boon against predators. Incidentally, human babies are covered in a fine, downy lanugo when they are in the womb but it is usually shed before or soon after birth.

When the time comes to give birth, females congregate on the shore in large groups called rookeries. Each female has a single pup. Several hundred mums and babies are crowded into a small area so there may be confusion in the melee. However, mothers don't tend to hunt while they are lactating and stay with their pups most of the time until they are weaned. Females have to rely on their fat stores to produce milk for their pup and mothers can shrink rapidly, losing about 3 kilograms a day. The mother's milk contains up to 60 per cent fat and pups grow quickly, putting on about 2 kilograms every day. Pups moult into their speckled grey coat when they are weaned at about 2 to 3 weeks old. Each seal has unique markings on their fur and we can recognise individuals. But can seals tell each other apart?

This is important because mothers and pups can sometimes become separated, perhaps during bad weather, or if the mum goes for a swim, or males are charging around the rookery fighting for mating rights. Males can weigh up to 300 kilograms so any pup that gets in their way may be crushed. However they become separated, mothers and their offspring need to be reunited or the pup will starve. Each mother and pup produce vocalisations such as growls and moans that are unique to each individual. Surprisingly, some playback experiments which played different pups' calls to mothers and monitored their reactions have concluded that grey seals don't always use these auditory clues to recognise each other. Perhaps other clues are more obvious. Pups don't move far so the mother can just return to where she last suckled and then use a combination of sight, sound and smell to track down her pup.

Saving for a Rainy Day

Do birds hoard food? I have been watching a coal tit for about an hour going to our bird feeder and taking sunflower kernels. It has not eaten any but has been very busy burying them in my flowerpots and carefully covering them up with moss. I am watching carefully to see if it comes back for them! I have never seen this behaviour before. Has anyone else? *Lindsay*

We are keen birdwatchers and we have a coal tit that appears to behave strangely. It is like a squirrel; it takes food from one of our feeders and then proceeds to hide it in the grass or soil. Is this normal for the coal tit or have we just got a strange one? *John*

Coal tits are prodigious hoarders but other members of the tit family, such as marsh tits, willow tits, crested tits and great tits, also store food to get through lean times. Coal tits cache food mostly between June and December, peaking just before their invertebrate prey of insects and grubs become scarce and when trees produce most seeds. The woodlands that coal tits inhabit – mostly pine, spruce and birch – have very variable and unreliable seed crops so it makes sense to store food while the going is good.

Coal tits will also make the most of a frequently filled birdfeeder, busily collecting seeds and hiding them around the local area. They are known as scatter hoarders because they have many small food stores rather than one big larder.

Seeds are tucked into crevices in tree bark, buried in the ground or hidden in any other nooks and crannies they can find, like Lindsay's flowerpots. Birds may hoard vast numbers of seeds and nuts when there is a good seed harvest. Siberian tits have been recorded as hoarding over half a million seeds a year per individual when there is a bumper spruce mast.

It's not just seeds and nuts that are cached, though. It is also useful to store food that is only available at certain times; for example, shellfish that are exposed just at low tide. Hooded crows sometimes cache mussels, burying them in grassland near to the shoreline to be eaten over the next few days. Tide times shift each day so the crows make the most of the low tides that coincide with daylight hours.

It's all very well hiding food to eat at a later date, but finding it again is a different matter. Coal tits and other scatter hoarders need to have a good spatial memory to retrieve their caches. Stored seeds are usually eaten within a few days, but laboratory experiments have shown that coal tits can remember the location of their cache for up to four weeks. This ability resides in a part of the brain called the hippocampus. The hippocampus is bigger in food-storing birds and it also grows at the time of year when it's needed for hiding and retrieving food. Nevertheless, scatter hoarders like coal tits, squirrels and jays won't remember where all of their stores are hidden and the plantworld will benefit from their forgetfulness. A jay may collect up to 5,000 acorns each autumn and bury them over a wide area. A large proportion won't be recovered and will grow into young saplings instead, and so by planting acorns and forgetting about them jays inadvertently help the spread of oak woodlands.

House Guests

Why do you get so many spiders in your house at this time of year? My wife keeps asking and all I can think of is the damp. *Fastfox*

There are about 650 species of spider in the UK but few venture into our homes. Spiders that apparently 'invade' houses during autumn aren't avoiding the weather or searching for somewhere warm, they are in fact looking for love. If you find an eight-legged friend scuttling across the carpet at this time of year, it is probably a male from one of the four species of *Tegenaria* house spider that are resident in the UK. The males can be recognised by their palps, which look like little boxing gloves attached to their head. The males also have smaller bodies than the females but longer legs, with a span that can reach up to 75 millimetres. They have a messy flat web with a funnel in one end where they lie in wait for their prey. House spiders often live unnoticed in your home, hidden away in some dark corner. They can survive for months with no food or water but the males become more visible in autumn when they are on the hunt for a mate. These males can get into trouble on their travels and are often found in slippery-sided baths and sinks, trapped until a kind human removes them.

During the mating season, the male will spin a small web and place in it a drop of sperm from an opening in his abdomen. He then sucks the sperm into his palps, filling them like water pistols. Next he needs to find a suitable female, one who is about to moult. As he approaches a web he can tell if the female is ready by her pheromones, chemicals that he can sense with his feet and palps. Once he finds a potential mate, the male must court her cautiously to ensure that she doesn't mistake him for prey. He sends her signals through the strands of her web by performing a mating dance. He taps the web with his palps and feet and bobs his abdomen up and down. From these movements the female can tell that he is a willing male from her own species. If she accepts him, the pair live together in her web until the female is ready to moult.

Immediately after the female moults and sheds her skin, the male mates with her, injecting the sperm stored in his palps into her abdomen. He stays by her side, guarding her from rival males and mating repeatedly because the female stores sperm until she is ready to fertilise her eggs the following spring. The male wants to ensure his paternity, so he will chase off any rivals that dare to approach the web. Sadly, the male doesn't survive the winter. Contrary to many myths, the female doesn't kill him but she may indeed eat his body after he dies. In death he provides extra nutrients for his future offspring. Next spring the female will produce several egg sacs, and a month or so later out of these will hatch tiny spiderlings.

House spiders may give you a fright as they scurry about on their romantic missions, but if left alone each house spider will provide the service of eating up to twenty flies per year. By letting them go about their business, house spiders will help rid your home of woodlice, small moths, cockroaches and other undesirables.

Completely Legless

This morning (18 October) I saw two newly hatched slowworms, each about 9 centimetres long, near my house in Cornwall. Is it usual for slowworms to hatch at this time of year? It seems very late and they appear to be very small to survive the impending winter weather.
Hilary

The first thing to point out about slowworms is their inappropriate name – they're not necessarily slow and they're not worms. Despite appearances, they're not snakes either. Slowworms are legless lizards that have lost their limbs through millions of years of evolution. Presumably this is because limbs are unnecessary for their burrowing lifestyle; they spend much of their time underground or moving through small crevices and tight spaces where legs may hinder rather than help. If you're in any doubt about whether the long, slithery creature you've found is a slowworm or a snake, take a close look at its eyes. If it blinks it's a slowworm – snakes don't have eyelids.

Unlike snakes, slowworms have very shiny small scales and don't have a forked tongue. They also have a clever trick that is unique to lizards, called 'caudal autotomy'. If threatened or caught by a predator, a slowworm can shed its tail and leave it wriggling on the ground while the front half makes a quick getaway. The tail will eventually grow back but not to its original length.

Like other British reptiles, slowworms survive the winter by hibernating during the coldest months. They often congregate to spend the winter in compost heaps. Slowworms are a welcome addition to any garden because they eat pests like slugs, caterpillars and small snails, gripping their slippery prey using sharp, backward-pointing teeth.

Slowworms emerge from hibernation in March and mate in May. Courtship may last ten hours and the male keeps hold of the female by biting the back of her head. Once the eggs are fertilised, it takes several months for the young to develop inside the female. Eggs would be vulnerable if they were laid too soon in our unpredictable temperate climate, so the mother retains the embryos inside her body where conditions are more consistent. In late August or early September a dozen or so tiny live young are born, just 7–10 centimetres long. They must fend for themselves and feed up ready to hibernate a couple of months later. Predators are a bigger threat than inclement weather and the young are particularly vulnerable to birds, frogs, toads, hedgehogs and cats. If they avoid these dangers the young slowworms may grow up to half a metre long and live for up to thirty years or more.

Tangled Web

In autumn you see some massive spiders' webs spun by orb weavers. I've seen one web spun between two trees some 2½ metres above the ground and the trees are roughly 2 metres apart with a small shrub between the two. The question I have is how does the spider get that first long line between the two trees? At first I thought it ran down one tree and then up the other, before pulling the line tight, but I can't see how it could do this without the line getting tangled up somewhere along the route. *Steve*

What do spiders do with their old webs? Having witnessed one rolling its destroyed web into a ball on our balcony before retreating to apparently rest, I am very intrigued to learn more about this fascinating behaviour which I had never observed before. *Ted*

A spider's web is an architectural wonder and one that is stunningly beautiful when bejewelled with dew or frost on an autumn morning. The classic wheel-shaped webs so often seen at this time of year are spun by orb spiders. A spider begins building by climbing to a high point like the end of a twig and letting out a fine silk filament that floats on the breeze until it catches onto something. Once the spider feels the filament become taut, it ties it onto the twig and runs across to the other side, laying a stronger line as it goes. Then it returns to the middle and drops another line to form a Y shape to anchor the structure. The spider then spins strong radiating spokes, attaching them to nearby anchor points. Next, it works in a circle to create a scaffolding spiral, progressing from the middle outwards. Finally, the spiral is embellished with many fine sticky strands and the scaffolding strands are eaten to be 'recycled'.

The whole web takes about an hour to construct. The process is a mammoth feat of engineering – the equivalent of a human building a structure the size of a football pitch which is tough enough to catch an aeroplane. Some species, such as wasp spiders, also make their webs stronger and more attractive to insects by decorating them with an ultra-violet, reflective zigzag pattern called a 'stabilimentum'. These appear to draw in insects that are sensitive to UV light, especially pollinators such as flies, beetles and butterflies.

Each web may contain up to 60 metres of silk of several different kinds, each suited to a particular job; from sticky strands to catch prey to the tough anchor lines and swathing silk used to wrap up struggling insects. In case you're wondering, spiders don't stick to their own webs because they know where the sticky parts are and so they make only minimal contact with them. Despite its delicate appearance, spider silk is incredibly strong and elastic. The fine, flexible threads of a spider's web can be five times stronger than a steel thread of the same thickness and up to ten times as strong as Kevlar, the material used in bulletproof vests. Students from the University of Leicester have estimated that a single spider's web of the Darwin's bark spider from

Madagascar could stop a Tube train travelling at speed if it was large enough and anchored well.

Usually the spider sits in the centre of the web, waiting for a hapless fly or other insect to become ensnared. It senses any vibrations from the web's threads and can tell the difference between a leaf, prey or a potentially dangerous wasp from the movements. Not only is spider silk very strong, but the web's design is inherently resilient – if one strand of the web is broken the structure becomes stronger not weaker. However, once a web becomes too damaged to repair, or loses its stickiness, the spider will roll it up and eat it so it can recycle the silk protein's building blocks to use in another web.

Many cultures traditionally used spider webs to treat wounds as they have antiseptic properties, help stop bleeding and aid healing. Modern scientists are trying to re-create spider silk for all sorts of human uses, including medical applications that would help to regenerate damaged cartilage or bone. It seems that Nature has created materials and designs that humans simply cannot match yet – even fictional superheroes like Spiderman have nothing on these creatures!

Small Talk

I would love it if you could put me out of my torment over ladybirds. How do they communicate? They don't appear to make any noise, yet they seem to get together in big groups. *Robert*

At this time of year, ladybirds gather in large numbers, often in their thousands, to hibernate through the winter. They huddle under tree bark or find shelter in our homes and sheds. There is safety in numbers – if the group is discovered by a predator then each individual has a greater chance of survival if there are several thousand ladybirds to choose from. Also, ladybirds taste unpleasant to most animals and once a predator has tried one it's unlikely to eat the others. So how do ladybirds organise these annual get-togethers?

Like most insects and bugs they rely on chemicals for communication. Ladybirds produce different pheromones that waft through the air and are detected by other individuals. There are specific pheromones depending on the situation and each induces a different response. For example, ladybirds release a particular scent when a good supply of aphids is discovered. The aphids also release an alarm pheromone that alerts other aphids that they are under attack, but this chemical also draws more ladybirds to the feast. An animal doesn't only respond to its own species' messages but can intercept and react to a predator or prey's scent too.

Each species of ladybird has a unique perfume, which means that it hibernates with its own kind. For example, the seven-spot ladybird (*Coccinella septempunctata*) produces a chemical called 2-isopropyl-3-methoxypyrazine. It might have a tongue twister of a name but the message to other seven-spot ladybirds is clear; when one ladybird finds a suitable place to spend the winter it produces this long-lasting aggregation pheromone that attracts other ladybirds in the vicinity. Scientists are only just beginning to decipher some of the complex chemical communication used by insects but, once understood, this knowledge could be very useful in controlling agricultural pests. Chemical lures could divert pests away from crops and save on the use of pesticides.

Autumn's Progress

Does autumn spread across the country from one end to the other? *Shaka*

A slightly glib answer is 'it depends on how you define autumn'. Some people believe the season begins at the autumnal equinox at around 22 September when there are equal hours of daylight and night. The Met Office defines autumn as the months of September, October and November; this allows meteorologists to compare weather conditions during those 'autumn' months over decades or longer. However, Nature pays no attention to the human calendar and so the biological signs of autumn vary from year to year and across the country. But does autumn begin when the trees turn brown, when migrant birds arrive, or the last time you mow your lawn? See? It's trickier to pin down than you might expect ...!

The study of how seasons progress is called phenology and Britain has a long tradition of naturalists keeping detailed seasonal records of plants and animals. This tradition is being continued by the Nature's Calendar project run by the Woodland Trust. It encompasses various surveys to which the public contribute by noting when biological phenomena occur – such as flowering dates, the first swallow arriving and other signs of the turning seasons.

Arguably, it's more difficult to study the spread of autumn than spring as the signs are often more obtuse. Some autumnal changes, such as leaf tint, are more subjective than bud burst or first flowering – it's easy to tell when a flower opens but not so obvious at which point a tree's leaves are changing colour. Fruits are easier to monitor; for example, when blackberries ripen or fungi emerge. So the progress of autumn depends on which signs are being studied.

The most important factors affecting how plants and animals change are temperature and day length. So it seems intuitive that autumn should arrive first in northern Scotland where temperatures are usually cooler and day length shortens quickly. Unfortunately, it's not quite that straightforward. For example, bird migration is triggered by day length but prevailing winds can affect when birds arrive on our shores. Unusual weather can also have an effect on which parts of the country feel autumn first. As a vast generalisation, though, autumn spreads southwards from the north, and spring moves northwards from the West Country.

As our climate changes, long-term phenology studies are increasingly important. Research shows that the timing of spring has shifted over the past few decades, with many plants coming into leaf and birds nesting a week or ten days earlier. This can have negative implications if various dependent species fall out of sync; for example, if a great tit times its brood to coincide with a glut of caterpillars. If great tits and their prey react at different rates to climate change they may become uncoupled and great tit chicks will go hungry. Biologists are just beginning to unpick and understand these relationships, so the science of our seasons has never been more pressing.

Loud and Proud

I have a burning question. This time of the year you see a lot of geese migrating and it has never ceased to amaze and tickle me that, while flying, the geese just never, and I mean NEVER, shut up! It's always HONK! HONK! HONK! I am more than a little curious if this noise carries on for their entire journey even when crossing the ocean, because surely making all that noise saps energy? *Gojira*

Geese have been reported flying as high as 6,000–9,000 metres when migrating. How do they manage this? If we were that high we would need additional oxygen to stop us falling unconscious! *Red Kite Girl*

About 700,000 geese arrive in the UK each autumn, including brent, barnacle, pink-footed, greylag and white-fronted geese. They fly thousands of kilometres from their breeding grounds, travelling across the Arctic Circle, Scandinavia, Iceland and Greenland to take advantage of our comparatively mild winters. Some species roost and graze in vast flocks of up to 30,000 geese or more. Predators are inevitably drawn to these bird buffets, but with many thousands of eyes looking out for danger they don't always get an easy meal.

Geese migrate in groups, flying in distinctive 'V' formations. Many small birds also migrate in groups but tend to fly in less ordered formations. So what's the advantage of flying in a V shape? Firstly, by flying in this formation each of the trailing birds can conserve up to 50 per cent of their energy compared to flying alone. This is because as a bird flies each wing tip creates a vortex of swirling air in its wake. Another bird flying nearby can take advantage of this uplift, much like racing drivers or cyclists try to exploit each other's slipstream. Of course, the leading bird makes no energy saving, but the geese take turns to fly at the front, swapping when they get tired, so that each one benefits. The V formation also makes it easier to keep track of each member of the flock and may help communication. Hence the honking. Geese regularly call to each other throughout the journey to keep the flock together and coordinate their movements. Who knows, maybe they're debating the best route? Honking expends a little extra energy, but the benefit of staying together makes it worthwhile.

Geese and swans are able to fly at extreme altitudes. Whooper swans have been recorded flying at 8,200m where the air temperature could be minus 40 degrees Celsius, but the high-flying record goes to bar-headed geese that migrate over the Himalayas at 9,375m – an altitude higher than Mount Everest. Humans struggle to breathe let alone exercise at these altitudes, where oxygen levels are so low, but swans and geese can fly with little problem. How can they perform one of the most energetically demanding activities possible with so little oxygen and in sub-zero temperatures? Firstly, geese are well insulated and flying generates a lot of heat. Secondly, birds' respiratory systems are much better adapted for operating at altitude than mammals. Humans and other mammals have 'dead-end' lungs that are inflated and deflated as the air goes in and out, like a pair of bellows, and thus fresh, incoming air is mixed with 'old' air. Birds, on the other hand, have circulatory lungs that are ventilated by a system of nine air sacs throughout the body. These air sacs don't extract oxygen but allow a constant flow of fresh air in one direction through the lungs. The lungs don't have 'dead-end' air sacs like mammalian lungs but instead have a network of tiny interconnected airways, providing a much more efficient method of exchanging oxygen and carbon dioxide. It is this sophisticated gas exchange system that allows birds to fly in such thin cold air.

Sonic Booms

Which bird has the loudest call? *Thomas, aged 6*

Cetti's warblers have a very loud, shrill call and the little wren has an extraordinary call given its size, but the loudest bird in the UK is the bittern, a very shy, rare, brown heron. The bittern lives in dense reedbeds where its beige and brown plumage makes excellent camouflage. If it feels threatened or senses that it has been spotted, the bird will point its bill skywards and freeze, merging into the surrounding reeds.

The bittern may be difficult to see but its call is unmistakable. Its Latin name is *Botaurus stellaris* – *Botaurus* refers to bellowing like a bull and *stellaris* means 'starry', reflecting its speckled plumage. The males produce a deep, resonant boom unlike any other bird in the UK – it's rather like the Barry White of avian romance! The call is described as sounding like a cross between blowing across the top of an empty bottle and a distant foghorn. Whatever it lacks in melody, the bittern makes up for with power. The low-frequency boom can exceed 100 decibels, louder than a motorbike engine, and can be heard by other bitterns up to five kilometres away. Bitterns are so elusive that few people have ever seen them making such an impressive call. Biologists do not yet fully understand the mechanism but think that bitterns gulp in large amounts of air and expel it again to produce the deep boom. A male bittern makes a succession of three to five booms in a 'boom train' and it is thought that the fittest individuals perform longer boom trains.

Like most birds, a male bittern calls to attract females, declaring that he holds a territory that can support a growing family. They call most frequently at dusk and dawn and each male has a distinctive voice. By analysing each call, researchers can gain a much more accurate picture of exactly how many males are booming in one area and so monitor their populations. This is imperative because the bittern's success in the UK has been on a knife edge. The species was declared extinct in the late nineteenth century due to hunting and habitat loss, but these birds re-colonised the Norfolk Broads in the early twentieth century and the population grew until the 1950s, until the bittern was nearly lost again a couple of decades ago. Now, with the aid of targeted conservation schemes and reedbed restoration, the bittern is making a slow but steady recovery. In 1997 there were thought to be just eleven booming males in the whole country, but that number has now grown to over a hundred males. With sustained protection and support, hopefully their population will continue to boom (!) and many more people will experience the pleasure of their bellowing calls.

Time for Bed

When do hedgehogs start hibernating? Is it only driven by the falling temperature? *Errandir*

Hibernation is an extreme solution to a perennial problem: a lack of food in the winter. Only three types of mammal in the UK truly hibernate: bats, dormice and hedgehogs. Dormice (from the French *dormir*, meaning 'to sleep') are known as the seven-month sleeper and may indeed spend up to three-quarters of their life curled up in hibernation. Other mammals, such as badgers and squirrels, may sleep more in the autumn than they do in the rest of the year but they are still active during the winter months.

Bats and hedgehogs both rely on feeding on insects and invertebrates; both are less plentiful in winter so there is a food shortage just at the time when most calories are needed by these animals in order to keep warm and function. Hibernation helps them to overcome this obstacle. Bats retreat into caves or buildings while hedgehogs create a snug nest of leaves and grass. During hibernation, the hedgehog's metabolism is vastly reduced to 5 per cent or less of its usual needs and it can survive on its fat stores for several months. The heart slows dramatically, the body cools to ambient temperature, and although their extremities may often be just above freezing, the heart and other organs will be a little warmer. If the air temperature falls below freezing the hedgehog can burn some of its brown fat to prevent frostbite.

Hibernation doesn't follow a set timetable but hedgehogs do need to reach a weight of about 600 grams to ensure they have enough fat reserves to survive until spring. Many hogs will remain active as long as food is available, and you can help by providing water and dog food (not bread or milk as this upsets their stomachs). Hedgehogs may not hibernate until December or January but it's still worth checking any bonfires before lighting them on Guy Fawkes celebrations around 5 November to make sure hogs aren't sheltering in the pile of wood. Temperature is thought to be important for triggering hibernation and hedgehogs begin building nests ready for hibernation once the temperature falls below about 16 degrees Celsius. The optimum temperature for hibernating hedgehogs is about 4 degrees Celsius; if it's much warmer or colder than this their energy consumption increases. Other factors, such as decreased day length and a lack of available food, may also have an impact.

During hibernation hedgehogs will wake up every week or ten days for a few hours but they will stay in their nest and go back to sleep. However, mild weather during winter can put hedgehogs and bats in danger by 'fooling' them into waking up more often and becoming active. They then waste vital energy raising their body temperature and looking for prey when there is little food to be found. If you find an active hedgehog that you think should be hibernating, contact your local wildlife rescue centre for help and advice.

An Angry Mob

I've seen crows and magpies harassing foxes when they're out and about in fields during the day – why would they do this? The fox doesn't appear to be any threat to them. *Bev*

Why do crows attack birds of prey? *Malcolm*

Potentially, there are two reasons why crows and magpies would attack birds of prey and foxes: they either regard them as potential predators or as competition. If the crows were scavenging on a carcass in the fields they would try to see off any fox that might steal their meal. Crows and magpies might pull on the fox's tail, or call at and generally annoy the fox until it slopes off, leaving the food for the crows. It's equally likely that the crows see the fox as a threat, because foxes are one of the few predators quick enough and wily enough to catch them.

Birds of prey such as buzzards are often harassed by crows because they're recognised as a predator, especially when the crows have young in the nest. Several crows may work together to mob a bird of prey, flying at them, calling and generally making their lives uncomfortable.

Mobbing is not a behaviour restricted to crows and magpies, though – even small songbirds will take on a much larger bird of prey if it threatens their chicks. Great tits have a specific mobbing call to rally the troops and urge them into action, which differs from their alarm call. Many birds that live in colonies, such as gulls and terns, will cooperatively mob a potential predator to protect their offspring. They become very vocal, dive-bombing the bird, fox or other predator, and may defecate on them or even vomit at their target. Clearly, this is highly unpleasant, but the chemicals in vomit or droppings can also cause damage to a bird's feathers, a risk that many birds of prey would not want to take.

Not only does mobbing distract or drive off the predator, it also alerts other members of the colony or flock to the presence of danger and encourages them to join in the attack. Many predators rely on stealth to hunt, so once they have been spotted and attacked they may as well give up.

Anything that looks like a predator can trigger this response, even if they pose no danger. Herons may be mistaken for a bird of prey and come under attack. Even a person who goes too close to a nest during the breeding season may be dive-bombed or worse – so a hat or umbrella may be necessary to avoid the droppings!

Mobbing behaviour continues outside of the breeding season, too. It helps the young learn to identify predators and shows them how to respond to a threat. Several schemes to reintroduce rare birds have suffered because the chicks have missed out on this learning and either don't recognise predators or don't know how to defend themselves. Biologists now realise they must find a way to pass on this knowledge to the chicks before they are released.

Varied Diets

Why are sparrows eating my house?! We have a roost of between 20–30 sparrows, which we feed regularly. Our house is made of soft, red, London clay brick which the sparrows peck at and appear to eat. They do this almost every day. What are they up to and how can we protect our walls? *Ros*

House sparrows are named after their habit of living near humans rather than because of a penchant for eating buildings! There are two possible reasons for sparrows eating parts of Ros's home. Sparrows live colonially and often choose cavities in houses for roosting or building a nest, so they could be trying to excavate a cavity. A more likely explanation, considering this is a year-round activity, is 'geophagy' – which literally means 'earth-eating'. Sparrows and other birds need grit or some other fine, abrasive particles to help them digest their food, especially hard seeds, because they don't have teeth with which to chew their food so they need another way to break it down. Grit is swallowed and held in the gizzard, a muscular pouch that grinds the prey or grain into smaller pieces. In sparrows, there is a high turnover of grit, with only a quarter of particles left after 24 hours, so they need to replenish the grit every day and take in more as their diet changes throughout the year from insects to tough seeds. Grit also helps to provide extra minerals that may be lacking from their diet, like calcium.

If their chosen source of grit is a problem for you, you could try to divert their attention by providing a container of clean, fine grit or coarse sand. Don't use the kind of 'grit' used to de-ice roads, though, as this contains salt. Some experiments have shown that sparrows prefer green, white and yellow particles over red and darker colours, so offering grit of those colours may tempt sparrows away from your red London clay house.

Sparrows aren't the only animals that have been seen eating buildings, though:

Recently we witnessed a red squirrel acting unusually in Aviemore. First, we observed the beautiful little creature crossing the village road in front of us; it then hopped onto the church wall and scurried along before dismounting in front of the church. It then made its way across to the church, stopping in front of the external sandstone wall at a place located adjacent to the church door, then it started licking the wall. My guess is that it was getting salts from the stone wall. Could this be the case? Alistair

Unlike sparrows, squirrels don't need grit or sand to break down their food but they do seek out scarce nutrients. In the same way that farmers provide man-made salt blocks for livestock to lick to improve their nutrition, many animals are attracted to natural salt licks for their mineral content. Animals require various minerals for bone and muscle growth, such as sodium, phosphorus, magnesium, iron and zinc. In cold weather, animals may be drawn to the salt used to clear icy roads, risking their lives for the sodium it contains.

Certain building materials, such as limestone and sandstone, can make attractive salt licks. Limestone is a sedimentary rock, formed over millions of years by the compression of ancient shells and skeletons of microscopic animals, so it is rich in calcium carbonate. Similarly, the fine grains of sand found in sandstone are often glued together with calcium carbonate and iron oxide, which might account for the squirrel licking those church walls. Traditional lime mortar contains high levels of calcium too. There are other sources of this vital mineral, though:

> *The squirrels in my garden have eaten an entire sheep's skull over the past twelve months. They actively looked for it when I moved it around. Why would they eat a skull? Crazy Owl*

Often, supposedly herbivorous or vegetarian animals will chew on bones or discarded antlers to extract calcium. Squirrels whose diets lack calcium are prone to developing metabolic bone disease, a condition that leads to lethargy, fits, brittle bones and even death. Red squirrels are usually vegetarian but they will take the occasional bird's egg. Grey squirrels, on the other hand, are often more carnivorous than people realise:

> *We were on holiday last week and where we were staying people regularly gave the squirrels nuts and so we could get nearer to them than usual. Sitting on the fence was a little squirrel nibbling away. 'Ah', we thought and went to get a closer look. I was horrified to watch it eat a robin, head first and down to tail feathers and legs, and it fed with such gusto in less than three minutes! I felt a little traumatised, I thought they only ate nuts and fruit? Purple Lavender*

Grey squirrels have a broader diet than reds and will happily scavenge a dead bird. They also have little difficulty catching and eating young nestlings or fledglings, so much so that there is debate about whether grey squirrels are partly to blame for the decline in woodland birds over the past few decades. Some bird species, such as blackbirds and collared doves, do seem to fair worse in areas with a high concentration of grey squirrels, but to date there is little evidence that they have a negative impact on overall bird populations.

Alien Invasion?

Can you solve the mystery of the jelly-like substance found in various places around the country this year? It looks just like wallpaper paste and is nothing like the inside of disposable nappies or the gel that you put in hanging baskets. I have already seen it again this year at the beginning of October on Dunkery Beacon and I usually see it where there are red deer nearby. My favourite of all the theories listed is deer semen – given that the rut is now in full swing. If you type alien snot or star jelly into a search engine, you will immediately find out what I'm writing about. *Sally*

I found some mysterious jelly-type stuff like frogspawn without the eggs in the heather/bog on the hills, near Snowdonia, when I was hillwalking this weekend. Really bizarre stuff. Had me stumped! *Jon*

Star jelly has been foxing people for generations. Lumps of a translucent or greyish gelatinous substance, like something out of a 1950s B-movie, have been found in various places across the country. Star jelly has mysteriously materialised on the top of fence posts, on the forest floor and even in the middle of a bleak moor. Over the years there have been many theories about what it is and where it comes from. For centuries, star jelly was thought to have celestial origins (hence the name) and people thought that these clots of slime fell to Earth during a meteor shower. The truth is only slightly less awe-inspiring.

Some of the confusion about the origins of star jelly is due to people lumping all reports of slime together. In fact, there are myriad different wobbly materials, each with a particular source. Man-made substances, like the gel from disposable nappies, explain some of the reports but many do have a biological origin. Any translucent white lumps found attached to dead wood are probably the crystal brain fungus (*Exidia nucleata*) or a similar species.

Slime moulds can also appear on dead wood, leaf litter and grass where they feed on tiny bacteria, fungi and yeasts. These fascinating single-celled organisms used to be considered fungi but now have their own classification due to their unique nature. Slime mould cells may aggregate to form shape-shifting blobs that can move around as a single body in search of food. They come in a variety of colours and shapes and some have gloriously descriptive names, like the dog vomit slime mould (*Fuligo septica*).

Another microscopic organism may be responsible for some reports of star jelly. A kind of blue-green algae called nostoc is made up of long filaments of cells encased in a gelatinous sheath. These lumps often go unnoticed but will swell up after rain into large green globules.

So certain types of star jelly can be attributed to nostoc, fungi or slime moulds. However, some examples that have been analysed contain no DNA, which means the blob is not a living organism or even misplaced deer semen. Could it be the remnants of a meteor fallen from the sky? In a word, no. These lumps of slime are often described as looking like frogspawn but without the black dots of tiny tadpole embryos, and that is exactly what they are. Female frogs encase their eggs in a clear glycoprotein gel that swells on contact with water. If threatened by a predator she may eject the jelly, or if she is eaten the oviducts may be regurgitated by the animal that caught her. These expand after rain to create mysterious star jelly, though 'frog jelly' might be a more appropriate name.

Late Breeders

Do pigeons usually mate in October? *Jenny*

Woodpigeons and feral pigeons both have a very long breeding season, particularly in suburban areas where a steady supply of food allows them to reproduce almost year-round. Most clutches are laid in spring and summer but they will lay eggs whenever there is enough food. They mostly eat grain and seeds, so in rural areas breeding often coincides with ripening grain crops.

Pigeons have a special method of feeding their chicks that is unique among British birds. Members of the pigeon family produce crop milk, a liquid that contains similar nutrition to mammalian milk. Both male and female parents produce the milk in their digestive system, which is high in protein and fats. The milk is made from fluid-filled cells that are shed from the crop's lining and regurgitated as a pale, crumbly substance that looks a bit like cottage cheese. Milk production begins towards the end of incubation and is stimulated by prolactin, the same hormone that triggers mammalian mothers to produce milk. The only other birds that produce crop milk are male emperor penguins and flamingos.

Young pigeon chicks are fed exclusively on this crop milk for the first few days after hatching. Like mammalian milk, crop milk contains antibodies that boost the young pigeons' resistance to infections and diseases. After a couple of weeks, the parents begin 'weaning' the chicks and feed them regurgitated grain that has been softened in their digestive system.

By producing crop milk, pigeons aren't tied to finding a particular food source, such as insects, for their young. The breeding season of other bird species may be restricted by the availability of suitable food, such as soft caterpillars, for the chicks. Pigeons, on the other hand, can turn any food they find into milk for their young and so can breed all year. When conditions are good, they can have six or more broods per year and a pigeon can start breeding at the age of six or seven months. This goes some way to explain how feral and wood pigeons have become quite so prolific.

Early Risers

Ramsons, also known as wild garlic, was out in the woods in Plymouth, Devon, today (30 October). Not just one plant, but many – poking up through the leaves. You could smell it as you walked through, and a couple of the plants were in full flower! This is at least five months early, isn't it? *Alison*

Wild garlic and other plants that grow from bulbs can become easily confused! Unlike other plants and animals that live above ground, they cannot take any cues from the shortening or lengthening days. Instead, they rely on the temperature of the soil to trigger their growth. As any gardener knows, putting a seed or bulb in the warm conditions of a cloche or greenhouse promotes their germination, and unseasonably warm weather can have the same effect.

Like animals that hibernate in winter, plants with bulbs can become dormant when the going gets tough, either when there is a lack of water or when temperatures drop. Wild garlic leaves usually appear from February to late spring, forming a dense, green carpet in ancient woodlands before the tree canopy shades out the sunlight. The leaves release their distinctive scent when they are crushed and are a popular wild food for foragers which can be used in soups, sauces and salads. The Latin name, *Allium ursinum*, meaning 'bear's garlic', apparently refers to the fact that bears also enjoy eating it.

The white star-shaped flowers bloom from April to June, and in around July the plant's resources are drawn from the leaves and flowers back into the bulb before the foliage dies off. The fleshy layers of the bulb are made up of modified leaves that act as a carbohydrate food store and fuel the next season's growth. In summer, decomposing garlic leaves create a nutrient-rich fodder for creatures of the woodland floor, such as springtails and woodlice. The bulb remains dormant until October, when roots begin to grow and new leaves are formed inside the bulb. When the temperature drops in winter, normally, the bulb becomes dormant again and the new, stored leaves will not emerge until the following spring.

Some plants' bulbs, such as tulips, require a long period of cold temperatures before they will grow. When the soil warms up (usually due to spring arriving) the shoots begin to push upwards. Unusual weather and fluctuating temperatures can 'fool' wild garlic bulbs into early growth in autumn. The plants that Alison saw in flower may be out of sync with their pollinating insects and so they probably won't produce as many seeds this season as they would in a normal year.

On the Move

Why do birds choose to migrate? Is it just because of food sources and cold weather or are there other reasons behind it? *Vicki*

Animals have various strategies they use to help them survive the hardest times of year: they can tough it out, sleep through it by hibernating, or escape the harsh conditions by migrating. Seeing as most birds can fly, many of these have opted to avoid winter altogether and head off in search of an easier life in warmer climes – and who can blame them!

Vicki hit the nail on the head. Most birds migrate because a food source becomes unreliable where they are currently living, usually due to cold weather. Swallows, martins and swifts leave us and head south to Africa for the winter where they can find a plentiful supply of insects. They are followed by hobbies, which eat insects too, but they are also partial to an in-flight meal of swifts or swallows to sustain them on their journey. Before modern ringing and radio-tracking studies, the annual disappearance of these birds was a complete mystery and many people believed that swallows hibernated underwater because they were often seen gathering around ponds. Their treacherous journey across the Sahara is no less remarkable and mind-boggling.

Many more birds join us in autumn, arriving from the north and east to exploit our mudflats, grasslands or berry crops. They come in all shapes and sizes, from massive whooper swans to minuscule goldcrests. Again, the thought of a tiny goldcrest being able to fly such large distances used to be so incredible that people believed they hitched a ride on the back of migrating woodcock, giving them the folk name of the 'woodcock pilot'.

Some birds migrate annually and have an inbuilt desire to head off at certain times of the year. They get the equivalent of itchy feet and experience an urge called 'zugunruhe' (from the German *zug* 'to move' and *unruhe* meaning 'restless') that is triggered by changing day lengths. Other birds will only leave home if forced; for example, waxwings will only fly to our shores irregularly, pushed across the North Sea when they run out of food in Scandinavia, which is a phenomenon called irruptive migration.

If life is so good here, why don't wintering birds stay in the UK? The migratory journeys are arduous and often dangerous, so the payback of migration must be worth the effort. You might wonder why birds such as brent geese bother to return to the Arctic to breed, but the tundra has plenty of benefits in the long summer days; there is more space and plenty of food for different species, the air is thick with a vast supply of insects and there is an abundance of lush grass.

However, it's not unknown for a species' migration to change and evolve over time. Blackcaps are usually a summer visitor to the UK, flying here from North Africa and the Iberian Peninsula to breed before returning in autumn. Likewise, blackcaps across northern Europe usually head south in autumn, but some German birds have begun to make a westerly migration and now spend the winter in Britain. Previously, any blackcaps that made their way here may not have survived the winter, but with so many people now feeding garden birds there is little chance of them starving. Blackcaps are very aggressive and will prevent other birds from using the feeders. (Tut, tut – banish all those stereotypes of beach towels and sunloungers from your head!) Our hospitality and warmer winters have led to increasing numbers of these winter visitors from Germany and we may even be changing their ecology. German blackcaps that spend the winter here can return to their breeding grounds two weeks ahead of birds that undertook the long journey to Africa. They tend to pair up with birds that wintered in the UK too, and breeding early may give them an advantage. These two populations of blackcap are separating and in time may become completely distinct species.

Feathered Friends

I have a couple of robins that visit my garden and they aren't afraid to get close to me if I have some suet sprinkles for them. I've heard of other people getting close to robins and even having them eat out of their hand. Are robins the bravest or most friendly of the garden birds? *Jadelyn*

The robin has been voted the nation's favourite bird and it seems that nearly everyone has a soft spot for this beguiling species. Robins not only look appealing with their fluffy red breasts and large black eyes but their trusting temperament endears them to us too. Robins are primarily woodland birds, but as gardening grew more popular in the eighteenth and nineteenth centuries many robins left their woodland homes, moved closer to our houses and into our hearts.

Of course, the affection mostly goes one way. 'Friendly' robins are simply exploiting us and our gardens for food and shelter. British robins are in fact tamer and friendlier than their European cousins. Over the generations they have adapted to the garden habitat and become far less timid near humans. The robin, also known as the ploughman's bird, will often keep gardeners company while digging, just watching and waiting for a juicy worm or grub to be unearthed. Their habit of sitting on the handle of an unused spade or fork handle, the cosy scene on countless Christmas cards, is just a variation on a natural hunting technique. A robin will find a high perch and scan the ground below, flying down to pick off any prey that appears. Before we became gardeners and farmers, robins would have followed wild boar rooting around on the forest floor or they'd forage around emerging molehills.

Although robins are 'friendly' with us, they are fiercely territorial and will fight other robins to the death. Still, our help can be crucial in the cold months of autumn and winter when food becomes harder to find. Many robins perish through starvation and only just over a quarter of robins will live for a year or more. Birds often become bolder with increasing hunger but robins are naturally confident and, with patience, one may summon the courage to eat from your hand. They particularly love mealworms and small pieces of cheese.

Solo Singers

We have a male blackbird that sits for hours in our pear tree on the house wall and sings very, very quietly but continuously to himself. Why is he doing this? *Ian*

On two separate occasions at this time of year, I have been in close proximity to both a robin and a blackbird. They were each singing their usual songs but with their beaks firmly closed, thus producing a muffled sound, clearly not intended for other birds to hear. Presumably, it wasn't for my benefit, so were they doing it for pleasure? *Graham*

Like all musicians, young songbirds such as robins and blackbirds need to learn and practise their songs before they perform in public for the first time. They may hatch with an innate framework of a song in their brain but a songbird must learn the details and embellishments from its parents, usually the father. There is often a critical time period for this learning; experiments conducted nearly 250 years ago showed that if a linnet chick was swapped into the nest of a skylark the chick acquired the song of its foster parents rather than its own kind. More recent studies have shown that when birds are raised away from their parents or other adults they will still sing but their song is much less complex, showing the importance of this early learning stage.

Chicks learn their songs in two stages. First they must listen closely and memorise the characteristics of the melody until they have a template in their mind. Then they must work out how to reproduce that song with their own vocal organs and practise it until it sounds right. Like children learning a language, the youngster will often try out notes and calls known as sub-song, the equivalent to baby-talk. The juvenile sings quietly to itself, listening to its own voice and honing the melody. It may take several months of trial and error for a bird to learn and rehearse the final adult song before it is ready to perform it.

Birds of the same species may sing with different 'accents'. Songs gradually change as they are passed from one generation to the next and this can give rise to local dialects. Birdsong can also alter over time in response to changes in the environment; for example, some urban birds now sing louder and at a higher pitch than their ancestors so they can be heard above the rising hubbub of the city. Studies on great tits have shown that city birds now have such a different song to their country cousins that they may no longer understand each other. It's more than just a different accent, it's like they are speaking another language.

A Hardy Bunch

It's the beginning of November, but I have seen three red admiral butterflies in the last four days. Should they still be about? I know our garden has never had so much bloom at this time of year, so could this be the reason why? *Vix*

It may come as a surprise to learn that red admirals are migrants to our shores. These striking butterflies with velvety black and red wings fly hundreds of kilometres from continental Europe every summer, an extraordinary feat considering their size and fragility. They begin arriving from March onwards and gradually move northwards across the country. The migrants lay eggs on nettle plants that later hatch into caterpillars. These pupate into a resident generation of adults that are joined by more migrants throughout the summer, reaching a peak in the population during September. The number seen each year depends on how many make the journey across the Channel.

Red admirals are quite resistant to cold and can be seen flying late in the year, often feeding on ivy flowers up until November. Garden plants also provide a much-needed sugar boost. Buddleia is a popular nectar source, but any late-flowering plants can offer a welcome meal. Red admirals also like rotting fruit such as blackberries and apples, so a later harvest will see them on the wing until the end of autumn or into early winter.

Until recently, red admirals were strictly summer visitors that would head south again in autumn. However, milder winters over the past couple of decades have allowed some adults to stay and survive the winter, especially in the south of England. Most resident butterfly species overwinter as eggs or pupae but some hibernate as adults, including the brimstone, peacock and comma, plus the large and small tortoiseshells. They often take shelter in our houses and garages but it's a risky strategy and many won't survive – they will succumb to freezing, starvation, predation or fungal infections if they hibernate somewhere damp. Red admirals don't go into proper hibernation like these resident species but simply roost during bad weather and emerge when conditions are fine. Red admirals seem quite hardy, though, and are commonly seen on mild winter days searching for a scrap of nectar. If the conditions are right, some may even breed in the winter and get a head start on red admirals migrating from Europe.

Going Nuts

We have a squirrel which is frantically yet randomly burying his nuts gathered from our feeder into various places in our garden – ranging from the borders to smack bang in the middle of the lawn and then, perhaps more understandably, around our newly created bundle of logs. Is our squirrel working to a set plan here or is he just working from instinct – surely he cannot remember where he's buried all of his nuts? *Wayne*

Both red and grey squirrels cache nuts and seeds in autumn when there is a surplus of food and will return to eat them at a later date. Grey squirrels may bury up to 3,000 acorns, beech nuts and hazelnuts each year and if they make all that effort to store food they must be able to find it again. Squirrels have a highly attuned sense of smell and biologists used to think that squirrels could simply sniff out their stored food rather than remember where they had buried it. However, experiments have shown that the process behind a squirrel's food choice and retrieval is much more sophisticated than you might expect.

First, they discriminate between which nuts to eat there and then and which to bury for later. The most perishable food items, or nuts infested with weevils, are eaten while more robust nuts are stored for later. In America, grey squirrels also 'process' their food, removing the embryos of a certain type of acorn to prevent them germinating while buried.

Squirrels and other hoarders often have their food stores pilfered by other animals so they become quite cagey if they're being watched. Squirrels may turn their backs or dig false caches to fool prying eyes. If they do bury a nut within sight of another animal, they often return later and move it to a new location when no one is watching.

Nuts are not buried in a random fashion. Squirrels have a good spatial memory and use landmarks such as trees, logs and bushes as markers for their buried food. Nuts don't need to be buried next to a specific landmark; squirrels can take visual cues from distant objects and are able to recover nuts even if they are hidden in the middle of an apparently featureless area like Wayne's lawn. Squirrels can remember the location of a cache to within a few centimetres and then use smell to pinpoint the buried nuts. Both reds and greys may cache food for over 60 days and still remember where it is. They often dig up their stores periodically and re-bury them elsewhere, perhaps to check the state of the nut, to refresh their memories, or to make sure it hasn't been stolen by another squirrel.

Royal Guard

Do all types of swans that live in the UK belong to the Queen? What about the ones that migrate here? Are they under the same protection? *Jo*

There are over 5,000 pairs of mute swans in the UK and they are the only resident species. In the winter they are joined by about 7,000 Bewick's swans from Russia and 11,000 whooper swans that migrate from Iceland. Historically, mute swans were a valuable asset, prized for their meat. Written records from 1186 refer to the mute swan as a royal bird, though the protocol probably existed well before that, and the ruling monarch could claim ownership of any unmarked mute swan in open water. The king or queen could also bestow ownership to favoured families or organisations. The royal privileges only apply to mute swans, though, not the two migrant species.

In theory, the Queen still has prerogative over any free-living mute swans in England and Wales. In reality, this only comes into effect on the Thames where the Crown is still regarded as the owner of any unmarked mute swans. Just three institutions other than the royal family own swans today. The colony at Abbotsbury in Dorset is owned by the Ilchester family, and two Livery companies, the Vintners and the Dyers, retain rights on the Thames along with the Queen.

In the past, owners needed to establish which swans were theirs, so each year mute swans and their cygnets were rounded up in a tradition called Swan Upping. During this annual rite, swans were marked by scoring patterns into their beaks which would identify their owner. This was done during the summer while the parents were in moult and the cygnets were too young to fly. As chickens and other poultry became more accessible, few people retained the right to own swans, and gradually the tradition of Swan Upping waned. Yet, the centuries-old Swan Upping still continues on a 126-kilometre stretch of the Thames between Sunbury and Abingdon, though. Members of the Vintners and Dyers companies plus the Queen's Swan Warden catch, weigh and examine the birds. However, these days the swans are counted, ringed and monitored for conservation purposes rather than culinary use.

All swans, their eggs and nests are protected by the Wildlife and Countryside Act of 1981 and it is a criminal offence to cause them any harm. Despite having legal protection across their range, Bewick's and whoopers have a hazardous journey to the UK. The Wildfowl and Wetland Trust has discovered that nearly a quarter of Bewick's swans and 13 per cent of whoopers that arrive here have been shot.

Mute swans have also faced problems. Monitoring on the Thames and elsewhere revealed a dramatic decline in numbers between the 1960s and 1980s. This has been attributed to the swans suffering lead poisoning after swallowing fishing weights. Now, lead weights are prohibited and numbers are recovering, but because the

Thames is a busy river the resident swan families there face many challenges posed by boats, dogs, discarded fishing tackle, overhead wires and the replacement of shallow, sloping river banks with sheer embankments. The 'quaint' tradition of Swan Upping continues its ceremonial purpose but also, more practically, helps to keep an eye on the fortunes of these birds.

Gravity-Defying Diners

We have a garden with dozens of birds on our bird feeders and there are lots of nuthatches on the fat balls all day long, but I want to know, why do they feed upside down most of the time? *Barry*

We have nuthatches that regularly visit our garden and bird feeders here in rural Oxfordshire. Can you tell me why they feed upside down? *Gillian*

Nuthatches, with their grey cap, black eye stripe and buff-coloured breast, are a welcome addition to our gardens, though they are quite aggressive and will see off most other birds at the feeder! They visit most frequently in autumn when their natural food sources diminish and they are forced to take advantage of the seeds and nuts that we provide. It is the only bird in the UK that can move down a tree trunk headfirst, and so nuthatches often adopt the same pose on bird feeders.

Nuthatches are superbly suited to tree-climbing. Woodpeckers and treecreepers that also scurry up tree trunks have long rigid tails that act like a third leg supporting their weight. Nuthatches have only very short tails and yet they can also move up and down freely. How? A nuthatch has 'scansorial' feet; that is, they're specialised for climbing by having large toes and claws to help them cling on. When going upwards, nuthatches move in a zigzag motion, keeping the centre of gravity on their lower foot. They move downwards more slowly, releasing one foot at a time. Nuthatches have a stout, sturdy beak that is used to pick bark off the trunk and search for invertebrates like insect larvae. They can also crack nuts by wedging them into a crevice and hammering them open. This habit of hacking open nuts probably gave rise to their name, which derives from the Middle English 'nuthak'.

So why would feeding upside down be advantageous? When they're not eating nuts, nuthatches tend to forage in the gnarly bark of oak trees, focusing on the lower and middle trunk. Their agility may allow them to reach areas of the trunk or branches that are out of reach of treecreepers and woodpeckers. Climbing down headfirst also gives them a different perspective, so they may spot a caterpillar or other prey that has been overlooked by treecreepers going in the opposite direction.

Nuthatches are gradually spreading northwards into Scotland, their progress aided by milder winters and people providing food in their gardens. Adult nuthatches remain close to where they fledge, though, so their range will expand slowly and they'll need more than full bird feeders to thrive. Each pair needs at least a hectare of mature woodland to provide enough food to raise a family, so protecting and managing forests is also vital for their continued success.

Autumn Quiz

1. If they have a lucky life, which of these animals lives the longest in the wild? Order them with the longest living first.

    A. Robin
    B. Hedgehog
    C. Mute swan
    D. Great crested newt

2. How many legs does a woodlouse have?

    A. 8
    B. 10
    C. 12
    D. 14

3. Which animals are known by these Old English or traditional names?

    A. Mouldywarp
    B. Sea Pie
    C. Brock
    D. Yaffle

4. Arachnophobia is a fear of spiders, but which animals would give you the jitters if you had these phobias?

    A. Ophidiophobia
    B. Chiroptophobia
    C. Ichthyophobia
    D. Apiphobia

5. Which of these is a real species of fungus?

    A. Poison pie
    B. Killer cake
    C. Death crumble
    D. Witches' tart

6. Birds of prey are also known as 'raptors', but what does the word 'raptor' mean?

    A. Claw
    B. To seize
    C. Dragon
    D. Sharp-beaked

Autumn Quiz Answers

Question 1 Answer:

C. Mute swan – their average lifespan is about 10 years but there are records of mute swans living for over 25 years in the wild.

D. Great crested newt – recorded living up to 14 years old.

B. Hedgehog – the average life expectancy is 2–3 years but they may reach up to 10 years.

A. Robin – most survive for just a couple of years but the oldest ever recorded was over 8 years old.

Question 2 Answer:

D. 14. Woodlice are crustaceans, more closely related to crabs, shrimp and lobsters than to insects.

Question 3 Answer:

A. Mole – derived from Germanic languages where the *mouldy* part means 'soil' and *warp* means 'throw', hence 'soil thrower'.

B. Oystercatcher – *sea* refers to where it is found and *pied* or *pie* meaning 'black and white', e.g. magpie.

C. Badger – from the Gaelic *Broc* meaning 'grey'. *Brock* in a place name is also thought to have a connection with badgers, such as Brockenhurst in the New Forest and the Ibrox district of Glasgow.

D. Green woodpecker – *Yaffle* is just one of the traditional, local names for the green woodpecker, which alludes to its loud, laughing call; others include *laughing Betsy*, *yappingale* and *woodhark*. Fans of the 1970s children's TV programme *Bagpuss* will remember the character Professor Yaffle, based on a green woodpecker.

Question 4 Answer:
A. Snakes
B. Bats
C. Fish
D. Bees

Question 5 Answer:
A. Poison pie. The scientific name is *Hebeloma crustuliniforme* and, as its common name suggests, the fungi are toxic.

Question 6 Answer:
B. To seize. The word 'raptor' comes from the Latin word *rapere*, meaning to seize and carry off or ravish.

Winter

What's the ultimate taste of winter? Nuts and Seville marmalade, perhaps? (Although it seems odd that Seville oranges turn up in January.) You just can't beat the taste of home-made marmalade, can you? The mass-produced stuff never gets close.

So, winter. First of all, of course, if it snows it is heaven for wildlife watching. You get an instant snapshot of what's going on out there. Fresh tracks in the snow sometimes tell a surprising story. You'll probably be amazed by the busy comings and goings in the garden. Sometimes a whole story unfolds – the hopping feet of a garden bird suddenly end abruptly, the imprints of splayed wing feathers in the snow, a trace of blood, bright red on white, marks the unmistakable kill of a sparrowhawk. I'm shocked to discover the fox has been patrolling around the edge of the chicken run, just inches away from the electric fence. Later in winter the prints of badgers and sometimes their cubs coming and going from the sett give a snapshot of their nighttime activity. It used to be thought that badgers hibernate over winter, and it was still being debated as late as the 1960s. However, research has shown that badgers do not actually hibernate, although they do slow down and may stay underground when it is very cold. You can see this for yourself if you visit your local badger sett after a fresh snowfall, where you will probably find footprints.

Winter is a good time to become a wildlife detective. If you find a fresh bird kill you can go all CSI and work out, from subtle clues, who the killer was. First look at the larger feathers, if the 'quills' at the bottom are bitten through the killer would be a mammal, perhaps a fox, weasel or cat. If the feathers are plucked out and the quills are whole, the killer will be a bird of prey. But which? If the body is mainly intact but the head is missing it is most likely a sparrowhawk. If more has been eaten, carefully examine the sternum (breastbone); if triangular chunks have been bitten out of it, it is most probably a peregrine falcon kill. Amaze your friends with your detective skills!

Look out for courting squirrels in late winter. Fortified by their stores of nuts (carefully put by in autumn), squirrels are often plump and very active towards the end of the season. Competing males can often be seen chasing teasing females up and down and round and round trees, accompanied by furious chatterings. Their agility is unbelievable and the chase joyous to watch.

Hedgehogs will be hibernating in winter, as one of only three types of animals that really hibernate in the UK, along with doormice (sometimes called 'seven-month sleepers') and bats. Our hedgehogs are in deep trouble but we can all do a bit to help by joining 'hedgehog street' (www.hedgehogstreet. org). The idea is so simple but so clever. Here's what you do – cut a small, hedgehog-sized, (15cm square) hole in the fence between your back garden and the neighbours. That's it! This simple act allows hogs to move between gardens. One small step, but the implications are enormous – there are no less than 23 million gardens in the UK, comprising nearly half a million acres. Start to join them together and you are creating a seriously significant habitat for wildlife. I love this idea. You can find out how to make your garden more hedgehog friendly at: www.lilacgrove.co.uk/hedgehogs-and-gardens/. This is written by my friend Duncan who has no fewer than 17 hedgehogs visiting his modest garden in Newport – so he knows what he's talking about.

The other crucial thing to do in winter – and all through the year for that matter – is feed your garden birds. I have my feeders set outside the kitchen and as I do the washing up a fantastic cast of colourful feathered characters play out their daily dramas. My life would be significantly less rich without my garden feeders. People often ask, 'can you overfeed garden birds?' and the answer is a categorical no. Birds are constantly at risk of predation and would never put on so much weight that it would impair their ability to escape. 'Fat' birds are very often cold birds that fluff up their feathers in an effort to keep warm.

An 'Unsprung' word for winter ... hmmm ... how about 'mandibulation'? This means the use of mandibles to manage food or nesting materials – you can see finches mandibulating seeds on your feeder.

One other thing you might consider doing in winter, which would certainly warm you up, is digging a pond. Now this is hilarious. I realised I did not know what time of year was best for digging a pond so I thought I had better look it up. When I did I discovered five different 'authorities' all suggesting completely different seasons of the year, each accompanied by careful reasoning. Five seasons? Surely there are only four? No ... one suggested winter as the pond would establish faster, one said autumn as the rains would fill it and it would allow time for the mud to settle. One said spring, one said summer – and another suggested a further 'in between' season, 'Late spring to early summer', as the best time to establish aquatic plants. So obviously you go ahead and dig your pond whenever it takes your fancy! My pond is an endless source of fascination to me; a stream of intriguing wildlife appears and emerges. I've seen animals up to the size of deer coming to drink from it too.

In a world full of over statement and hyperbole there is one final UK winter wildlife spectacle that I would say is the greatest, most astonishing I personally have ever seen – or heard. It's the huge starling 'murmerations' you can find all around the country. Even though our starling numbers are falling they swell in winter with migrants from Europe. To see and hear these gigantic flocks, throwing fabulous shapes in the sky, is mind blowing. And the sound as tens of thousands of starlings sweep overhead is like nothing else on Earth. It had been explained to me over and over again but I still don't really understand how they all turn so beautifully together without the mother of all pile-ups. Starling murmerations, if you haven't experienced one, are an absolute 'must see' before it's too late. It's one of the greatest wildlife spectacles in the UK, perhaps in the world.

Play Time

I think crows play. Our local crows often repeatedly slide down the roof of my house on sunny mornings, chuckling to each other as they do it. I've watched them and have never seen any point to it except as showing off to the other crows. *Gill*

The concept of animals playing has always been a bit controversial. For a start, it's quite difficult to define what constitutes play when analysing an animal's behaviour, although most of us recognise playful behaviour when we see it. Many biologists would argue that all behaviour has a purpose – animals don't play just for fun. There must be some benefit to play as it does have costs and potential dangers; for example, play uses up valuable energy and animals may be injured or become unaware of predators sneaking up on them while they are distracted. For these reasons it tends to be animals of a higher social status that are most often seen playing; hungry, tired or stressed animals don't have the energy or resources to spare. So, how do animals benefit from larking about?

Well, there are several theories about the function of play. Firstly, young animals need to acquire certain skills in order to be a successful adult. Predators need to learn how to hunt, prey animals need to be quick and agile to avoid their predators, and social animals need to establish the hierarchy – a fox cub that play-fights or stalks blades of grass is honing skills that will be needed later in life. There are dozens of possible other benefits of play, from simply releasing endorphins (i.e. for 'pleasure') or developing hand-eye coordination, to building useful social bonds (making friends) and diffusing any group tension. Clearly, no single theory can explain all types of play.

Intriguingly, there is evidence that play physically shapes the brain, preparing it for the demands of adult life. In animals, play tends to peak during puberty, when the brain is building connections. If a social animal such as a rat is reared alone with no playmates it cannot deal with difficult social situations later in life and so either becomes very aggressive or runs a mile. In the wild, the rough and tumble of play seems to inoculate animals against social stress; the adrenaline rush of chasing or play-fighting with another animal may mould how an individual reacts to a stressful experience and allow them to recover more quickly from it. Play can also make animals cleverer by stimulating the brain cortex to grow and make more connections. Young rats that interact with others and play with interesting objects develop bigger brains and learn more quickly.

Does any of this explain why crows might spend time sliding down a roof? Well, members of the corvid family are bright, social birds. Ravens and crows often perform aerial acrobatics on a windy day and there are many accounts of them sliding down muddy banks or 'sledging' in snow. Several theories may explain this behaviour in evolutionary terms: perhaps they're trying to impress potential mates, keeping fit or building their brains, but it's doubtful that the

crows themselves would be fully aware of those benefits.
Ask yourself, why would you go sledging?

Unusual Playmates

I am quite worried about the local foxes. I live in central London and they have not hibernated and have now started mating. Well, I think they are the cause of all the noise. Also, if I take the dog out late at night there is a young fox that plays with him. Reg the dog chases the fox – they run round in circles, and when Reg stops and sits down the fox sits down behind him. Then, when Reg has had a rest, they start again. As Reg is now 14 he doesn't play for that long. The foxes have been playing with him for the last three years and the fox always wins. Is this normal behaviour, and if we have a sudden cold snap will it affect the foxes? *Lesley*

Don't worry, foxes don't hibernate so it's perfectly normal for them to be active all winter. They grow a thick coat for extra insulation and are very resourceful scavengers and hunters. Foxes are hardy creatures and can still hunt when there's a thick blanket of snow – their sensitive hearing is able to pick up the sounds of a scurrying vole or mouse hidden underneath. Red foxes are widespread across the globe and can live in much harsher conditions than a UK winter – from the icy wastes of the Arctic tundra to arid areas of North Africa and the Middle East.

Foxes make dozens of different calls, such as barking to keep in touch with each other, but at this time of year they reach a crescendo. Winter is the mating season for foxes and they can be very vocal about it! Vixens in particular make an almighty racket, letting out bloodcurdling screams that can be easily mistaken for something more sinister on eerie December and January nights. Males may also scream occasionally, but vixens are fertile for just two or three days so they need to let the dog foxes know when they are receptive and how they can find them.

Young foxes also disperse in winter, leaving home to find a territory of their own and perhaps meeting dogs like Reg. Foxes are social animals and play-fights or chases are common within the group. Playing with other species is rarer, but we have received charming footage of foxes chasing about with dogs and even hanging out quite happily with cats. Perhaps this is not so surprising given that foxes and dogs are both members of the canid family and display similar behaviour patterns. Presumably, they are able to recognise and understand each other's body postures, such as the play bow when a dog or fox crouches down on its forelegs and raises it rear end – apparently this is the international symbol for 'Let's lark about!'

Boxing Clever

Inspired by your live minicams, I bought a bird box and put a small camera inside. Where is the best place to put it in my garden? *Charlie*

Where is the best place in the garden to put my bird box? I have a feeder as well but they are next to each other and I'm not getting a lot of activity. *Macbow*

With a shortage of natural nest sites, man-made homes can offer a lifeline to many birds. There are thought to be nearly five million nestboxes in the UK – a huge contribution to avian housing stock. There are some general guidelines for putting up a nestbox, but every garden is different so it may require a bit of trial and error before birds take up residence. Try to get inside the mind of a nesting bird: what does it want? Shelter and safety are the most important factors. Avoid positioning boxes in exposed places that will be hit by wind, rain or direct sunlight, and face the openings away from prevailing weather. Angle the box slightly downwards so rain won't get into the entrance. Make sure that the location is safe from cats or other predators. Woodpeckers and squirrels often attack nestbox entrances so you may want to reinforce the hole with a metal plate.

There is a wide variety of boxes designed to suit different birds. Robins and wrens like open-fronted boxes while tits and other birds prefer enclosed boxes with a small entrance. House sparrows and starlings nest communally so they will need several nestboxes scattered around in the same vicinity. Other birds prefer to keep away from their own kind so, unless your garden is large, it's best to offer different types of boxes to accommodate a range of birds. Spread them around the garden to give each pair some elbow room and reduce competition. There are more specialised designs and requirements for species such as barn owls and birds of prey, so do take advice if you think you can offer them a home.

If attaching the box to a tree, use a strap or wire rather than nails, which might damage the tree. Most birds will appreciate a clear flight path to the entrance with a few twigs or small branches nearby where the fledglings and adults can perch. Birds like robins that nest in open boxes prefer to have some cover such as ivy or bushes to hide the nest from predators.

There are plenty of designs for nestboxes online or in books if you're a dab hand at woodwork and fancy building your own. If you do go for a DIY nestbox, make sure you drill drainage holes in the bottom, use wood that is not too smooth so the chicks can scramble out when they are ready to fledge, and don't use paint or varnish because it may contain noxious chemicals. Untreated wood should be fine but a coat of linseed oil may help to waterproof the box.

As Macbow discovered, birds don't like to nest near feeders as there is just too much activity and they may spend fruitless hours trying to keep other birds out of their territory. Try moving the feeder (or the box) to prevent any conflict and to encourage a nesting couple to set up home. It may take a couple of years for boxes to be used; if they continue to remain empty, try moving them to a new location – somewhere that looks like an ideal nest site to humans may not be seen the same way by birds. With luck, patience and a relatively cheap nestbox camera you'll be able to follow the daily dramas of a bird family in your very own version of *Springwatch*.

Nocturnal Singers

Walking home from a night out in Croydon, at about 2am in the morning and in the dark, I heard robin song. Do they always sing so late into the night? *Sally*

At 3am the other night in York, I heard one solitary bird in full song – a robin. Why does it sing in the night? *Helene*

Several species of bird will sing at night. The most notable nocturnal serenades are sung by nightingales, though they will have headed for Africa by the winter. The mechanical churrs of nightjars and corncrakes are definitely less tuneful and they both migrate south at the end of the summer too. The sweet songs of blackbirds and robins are often heard in the hours of darkness, though blackbirds usually save their voice until spring, leaving just the robin's mellifluous tune to pierce the cold nights. Robins are territorial all year (see the earlier question on why robins have red breasts) so they continue singing into the depths of winter.

Incidentally, have you ever wondered why birdsong peaks during the dawn chorus, just as day breaks? There are a couple of reasons for this: by singing at dawn, a bird is declaring that he (it's usually males that sing) has survived the night and is still intent on holding his territory. The air is often calm and still at dawn so sound travels further. Also, birds wake up early before it is light enough to find food so they may as well sing. The dawn chorus reaches a crescendo during May when migrants have returned to breed.

Each member of the avian orchestra pipes up in a broadly similar order as the dawn progresses. Those with the largest eyes are well suited to the low light of dawn and dusk so they're often the first and last birds to be heard in the day. Robins, thrushes and blackbirds are literally the early birds that catch the worm; these songsters are the first to get out of bed because earthworms (their favourite food) are nearest the soil surface early in the morning. Birds such as goldfinches, chiffchaffs, wrens and blackcaps join the cacophony a little later because they have smaller eyes and mostly eat insects or seeds. Insects need warmth and only become active later in the day, so birds that feed on them may as well have a lie-in.

So robins are among the first to sing in the morning, but why would they bother to sing at night? Well, sometimes birds are startled into song by a loud noise or disturbance, but that doesn't explain such a widespread phenomenon. Many reports, like those of Helene and Sally, come from towns or areas with street lamps. At first it was assumed that robins, blackbirds and other species that were heard at night had been 'tricked' into singing by the artificial light. However, recent research suggests that robins are actually choosing to sing at night because cities and towns are just too noisy during the day. At 2 or 3 am, most humans are finally asleep and have stopped making a racket. By working a nightshift, robins take advantage of the quiet streets to make themselves heard, when just a few nightclubbers and fellow night owls are still awake to appreciate their song.

Bee Cool

Please can you tell me what bees do in winter? Do they hibernate or hoard? *Elaine*

Is it unusual to be seeing bees of the small fluffy variety in the garden already? *Nikrow*

Like many insects, bees hibernate through the coldest months when there is a shortage of food. Honeybees are domesticated, originating from southern Asia, and are particularly vulnerable to our chilly winters. At this time of year they retreat to the hive where they huddle together for warmth. The honeybees' yellow fur provides some insulation but they can also generate heat by vibrating their wing muscles. Individuals rotate inside the hive so that the bees on the cold, outer edge of the cluster get a chance to move into the middle and warm up. The colony lives off its honey stores until nectar becomes available again in the spring.

Native bumblebees (presumably the small, fluffy variety that Nikrow asks about) are hardier than honeybees. There are 24 species of bumblebee in the UK and young queens produced at the end of summer fatten up on nectar and pollen to get through the winter. Like hedgehogs, they must reach a certain weight to survive hibernation, about 0.6 grams for the buff-tailed bumblebee (*Bombus terrestris*). When they reach this weight they burrow underground and hibernate alone, living off their fat stores. If temperatures drop too low, a natural anti-freeze called glycerol is produced, which prevents any ice forming in the queen's body. Usually the queens don't emerge until the spring, when temperatures rise during February or March. Bumblebees can fly and start to forage when the air reaches 9 or 10 degrees Celsius.

However, since the 1990s one of the commonest species of bumblebee has become much more visible in the coldest months. In some places, the buff-tailed bumblebee is remaining active throughout the winter, even during freezing weather and snowy conditions. Most sightings are in the south and west of England, though they have been spotted as far north as Hull. This change in the bees' behaviour could be due to warmer winters, especially in towns and cities where temperatures are a few degrees warmer than in the surrounding countryside. Also, some buff-tailed bumblebees are imported from mainland Europe and used to pollinate commercial crops in polytunnels and greenhouses. These migrant workers are chosen because they tend to stay active for longer. Some sightings might be escapees, but these foreign bees may also be hybridising with native ones to produce a cold-resistant variety.

Whether native, foreign or hybrid, the bumblebees still need to find food – a warmer climate alone won't sustain them. Winter bumblebees aren't seen in places such as Brittany that have similar weather, and so seem to be a peculiarly British phenomenon. In fact, the bees' change in lifestyle may be explained by our passion for gardening; nearly all sightings come from urban or suburban areas where many of our flower-rich gardens now provide nectar all year round. Winter-flowering shrubs, such as mahonia, are becoming popular, and bumblebees may also visit winter honeysuckle, clematis and heather plus bulbs such as snowdrops and crocus. It just goes to show that the choices we make in the garden centre can make a big difference to wildlife.

Let's Go Fly a Kite

Today while driving at the edge of Savernake Forest in Wiltshire at about 4pm we saw a large number of birds circling in the sky above us. On closer examination we realised that we were watching at least 25 red kites! We have started to see increasing numbers of kites in this area but never in such numbers – why would they be circling together as a group in this way? *Dave*

Not long ago, the sight of 25 red kites soaring together would have been unimaginable. The return of red kites is one of the greatest conservation success stories of the past few decades. For centuries these scavengers were mistakenly regarded as a threat to game and livestock so they were persecuted, hunted and poisoned almost to extinction. By the 1800s red kites had been exterminated from England and Scotland, while just a few pairs clung on in mid Wales. At the turn of the twentieth century, concerned bird lovers and landowners began to protect the Welsh kites. Gradually their numbers grew; however, their rarity made them a target for illegal egg collectors and up to a quarter of nests were robbed each year. Nest protection increased in the 1950s and 1960s but it became clear that this small population of red kites would not be able to re-colonise England and Scotland.

A reintroduction scheme began in 1989 that brought birds from mainland Europe and released them at several sites in the kite's former range. By 1992, these birds were breeding successfully, and since further reintroductions over the past two decades red kites have now spread throughout much of the UK. In fact, they have now become so numerous that their population can only be estimated and is currently thought to be around 1600 pairs.

Attitudes have changed so much that red kites are now a tourist attraction, with several feeding sites across the country drawing in members of the public as well as dozens of kites. Hundreds of birds may travel to make the most of these artificial feeding stations and that may explain the appearance of big groups of kites. However, it's not just food that brings red kites together; they are often gregarious, especially in winter when they gather to roost in large numbers. At dusk they might be seen circling, soaring and chasing each other before settling down for the night, especially in windy weather when the air currents make their flight appear effortless. There may be several advantages for roosting communally, including the fact that many pairs of eyes are looking out for danger and they are able to follow others to a good food source in the morning. Adults leave the communal roost in spring to begin nesting, but young and non-breeding kites may continue to roost together throughout the year.

Red kites will scavenge on a wide range of food and may even hunt the occasional small rabbit if they are hungry. In winter, earthworms make up a large part of their diet, but there are other birds of prey that rely on worms too:

> *I live on the coast in Cornwall and about a month ago I was driving down one of the lanes when I saw about 30 birds flying above my head. I thought for a moment they were rooks but as I got closer I realised they were buzzards. I stopped below the circling birds, and right next to me was a tree which was also full of buzzards. I have only ever seen them in pairs, or family groups. Can anyone explain why there would have been so many of them in the tree and flying above? Drucilla*

During the winter months buzzards often congregate around good worm sites such as damp pastureland. Dozens of buzzards may tolerate each other in a freshly ploughed field full of worms. It can be quite surreal to see a large bird of prey grubbing about in the soil for a seemingly pitiful meal, but the buzzard's varied diet helps it get through the hard times of winter. Buzzards also have a long gut compared to other birds of prey, which allows them to extract as much energy as possible from relatively poor food. In fact, worms are full of protein and in wet weather they may be easier to catch than small mammals. They may not appear as appetising as a juicy rabbit or vole, but worms are a good source of sustenance.

A Worm's Woes

During floods, do worms drown? *Carolyne*

Worms respire through their moist, mucus-covered skin and don't have lungs or gills like other creatures. Oxygen and carbon dioxide diffuse in and out of their body as needed, and this process can happen in water or air, which means worms can survive in saturated soils for a long time, providing there is sufficient oxygen in the water. They can tolerate being submerged for several days, and at the other extreme, if soil becomes very dry, worms can dig deeper to find moisture or curl up in a burrow lined with their own mucus and wait for rain.

So why do so many worms come to the surface during or after wet weather if they're not trying to escape death by drowning? Usually, worms only come above ground at night when the air is cool and humid, plus there's less chance of being spotted by a predator. Some, like the lob worm, emerge to forage on leaf litter, and their nocturnal habits explain the old folk name of 'nightcrawler'. (Worms cannot see but they do have a light-sensitive organ that can distinguish between day and night.)

Worms may risk coming out during the day if they sense danger; they can feel the vibration of raindrops hitting the ground and may mistake it for the movements of a hunting mole, so they emerge to avoid being eaten. This tendency to head upwards is exploited by worm charmers and stamping birds that try to replicate the vibrations in order to lure worms to the surface. Another factor is that rain makes it easier for worms to leave home because they need damp conditions to migrate. If a worm wants to travel any distance it takes much less effort to move overland than to burrow through soil, so they take their chances above ground. There are also reports of earthworms 'swarming' in large groups; recent research showed that worms like to stick together, communicating through touch, and they may make group decisions to migrate in a certain direction.

Why do worms need to migrate? For a start, the ground under our feet can get pretty crowded. There are about 27 species of earthworm in the UK and rich soil may contain over 400 worms per square metre. However, the main reason for a worm to leave its patch is to hook up with a partner. With so many worms around it might seem easy to find a mate in the mud, but some species prefer to surface for romance:

A strange sight this morning – it was daylight, 8.15am,
about 8 degrees. Seven pairs of worms were copulating on
the surface of one field when I was out walking. Surely a
field day (literally) for the blackbird. The worms were head
to tail, with secretion from their bands, but their bands
were not together. On closer inspection (sorry, worms) they
sprung apart and popped down their respective worm holes.
Do they pop their heads above the surface, have a quick
look around for a partner, and if lucky start to procreate?
Luxintenebris

A worm may just stick its head up and mate with its nearest
neighbour, but by seeking a partner above ground a worm is
more likely to mate with another from further afield. Their
offspring would benefit from a greater genetic diversity so
it's worth the risk of travelling to find a partner. Worms are
hermaphrodites, each having male and female parts, so
when one worm meets another they glue themselves
together with a sticky substance secreted by their band, or
clitellum. They join up heading in opposite directions, as if
head to toe. The pair may mate for a couple of hours,
passing sperm to each other before going their separate
ways. Later, each worm produces a cocoon from its band
that contains fertilised eggs. The resulting embryos develop
inside the cocoon and hatch into tiny worms, vital for the
health of the soil.

Most people don't give earthworms a second glance, but
these unsung heroes enrich the soil by recycling nutrients,
and in so doing they aerate the soil and improve its
structure. As if that weren't enough, worms are high on the

menu for birds, moles and badgers. Indeed, Charles Darwin was fascinated by earthworms and claimed that few animals had a more important role in the history of the world. No one should underestimate the humble worm.

Getting a Head Start?

I saw blue tits going in and out of our nesting box in January. Does this mean they are breeding earlier?
Loopyloo

It's unlikely that these blue tits would be nesting as early as January. Blue tits generally have just one large brood a year and need a huge amount of caterpillars, spiders and other invertebrates to feed their growing family. This prey is simply not available in winter and so blue tits rarely lay eggs before mid-April. The blue tits may have been checking out the nestbox, though, to see if it would make a suitable home later in the year.

Nestboxes aren't just useful for raising chicks; they also provide refuge for adult birds during winter. Many birds, not just blue tits, seek shelter in nestboxes overnight, especially in urban areas and gardens that are a little warmer than the wider countryside. Birds will sleep in tree cavities, cosy crevices of buildings and specially constructed roosting pouches as well as nestboxes. Birds may choose to roost in nestboxes over other options because an enclosed box is better at retaining heat and is protected from wind.

A survey by the British Trust for Ornithology asked householders to note the roosting habits of various garden birds to see where they spent the night. Some species, such as blue tits and great tits, preferred nestboxes and liked to sleep alone. Others were more sociable and roosted in large groups. In this case, the old adage of 'birds of a feather flock together' is true and bedfellows are restricted to members of the same species. Even birds that are very territorial during the breeding season, such as robins, will huddle together for warmth on cold winter nights.

The wren, one of our smallest birds, often roosts en masse to conserve heat and save energy. It holds the record for the biggest sleepover: 63 wrens were squeezed into one (doubtless very cosy) box. It must have been quite a crush, reminiscent of world record attempts for the greatest number of people to fit in a Mini!

There is a downside to roosting in nestboxes, though. Parasites such as fleas may lurk in old nests and diseases may spread when birds are in close confinement. Still, the benefits outweigh these potential problems. By roosting in nestboxes rather than trees, birds may reduce their overnight energy use by 10 per cent, or even more if joined by friends. This may not sound much, but small birds barely have enough fat to make it through the coldest nights so any energy saving is a bonus.

Wrong Footed

Why do so many feral pigeons have deformed feet?
Terry

It's a common sight in many city centres – pigeons hobbling around on manky feet or even distorted stumps. There are several potential causes. Some city birds may get thread, fishing line or wire caught around their toes which eventually cuts off the circulation until the toes fall off. Feral pigeons also seem to be particularly prone to a condition known as bumblefoot, which is more precisely called ulcerative pododermatitis. Constantly walking on hard surfaces can cause small cuts and abrasions on the feet which are then susceptible to infection. Staphylococcus bacteria, found in the pigeons' droppings, then enter these wounds and cause abcesses or other problems. Affected pigeons seem to survive quite well as there is so much food easily available in the city, but their feet certainly don't look pleasant!

Pigeons aren't the only birds to have issues with their feet. Other species may develop foot problems caused by infectious diseases. Avian pox can cause wart-like growths on various parts of the body, including feet. Chaffinches in particular suffer from a disease called papillomavirus, similar to human warts, that leads to deformed feet. Another condition called tassel foot is due to a tiny burrowing mite that irritates the skin, causing tassel-like growths on legs and feet. Birds with these conditions may be lame but most seem to carry on despite any discomfort. However, you can help limit the transmission of these and other more serious diseases by regularly cleaning your feeders and birdbaths. Use a suitable disinfectant and rinse well to remove any residue before leaving to dry. Most bird diseases can't be caught by humans but birds may carry *E. coli* and *Salmonella*, which can both make us very ill, so it's advisable to use rubber gloves and wash your hands thoroughly after handling bird feeders.

Tail Story

What is a beaver's tail made of and what is its use?
Kristin

A beaver's tail is one of its most distinctive features – long, scaly and flattened like a spatula. It is made of bone, muscle and connective tissue covered in a thick, hairless skin. Historically, the beaver's tail was part of its downfall; beavers were hunted for their castor sacs, located just under the tail, which secrete a pungent-smelling substance. Beavers mix this with urine to mark their territories, but castoreum was valuable to humans for its use in perfume and as a food flavouring. Beavers were also hunted for food – as they swim and their tail has a fish-like appearance they were classified as neither flesh nor fowl and could be eaten on fast days.

The strong and muscular tail has a variety of physical and metabolic uses. It provides propulsion and acts as a rudder when swimming. Beavers often swim while dragging cumbersome branches or vegetation through the water; not an easy manoeuvre, but they can compensate for any one-sided drag by steering with their tail. If a beaver feels threatened it will slap its tail loudly on the surface of the water to warn others before promptly diving out of sight. The sound travels well above and below water and may also let any predator know it has been spotted or scare off whatever has upset the beaver.

In winter, the tail is used as a fat store, allowing the beaver to draw on extra calories if the food cache of submerged wood doesn't meet all its needs. In summer, a beaver's thick fur can be too warm so the exposed tail helps them to regulate their body heat. Beavers can't just hang out in the water when it's hot; they may need to come ashore to find food or maintain their dams. If a beaver is busy and building up a sweat on land it can stay cool by keeping its tail in water, even when the air temperature reaches 25 degrees Celsius.

On land the tail can act as an extra leg, providing support or balance when a beaver is propped up on its back legs gnawing on a tree or while using the special grooming claws on its hind feet. Finally, there's a slightly more unsavoury use for the tail ... Beavers, like other rodents and rabbits, are caecotrophic – they ingest green faeces and pass food through their gut twice to extract as many nutrients as possible. The tail makes a handy plate for eating these green faeces as they emerge. Nice.

Getting Cold Feet?

Do herons and other waders get cold legs when they stand still for ages in cold water? How do they overcome this? *Carol*

Why do some seabirds and wildfowl stand on one leg?
Ellen

Herons, waders, ducks and many other birds do get cold legs when they stand in water or on icy ponds. This isn't a problem for them, though. Firstly, their legs and feet aren't fleshy like ours; instead, they're made up of bone, tendon and scaly skin with few nerves to 'feel the cold', and the muscles that move their feet and legs are high up, near to the warmth of their body. However, the feet of ducks and waders can have a large surface area and have no insulation, so potentially a bird could lose a lot of heat through them. As ever, Nature has come up with a neat solution.

Ducks and waders have a counter-current heat exchange system in their legs. This may sound fancy but it's quite simple. A fine network of interwoven blood vessels transfers body heat from the warm blood descending the legs to the cold blood coming up from the feet. Basically, birds are able to warm blood coming up the legs by exchanging heat with blood coming from the heart. This is a win-win situation; it prevents cold blood shocking the system or bringing down the bird's core temperature and reduces the amount of energy lost through their feet. Species that live in colder climates tend to have more intertwining vessels so the heat exchange is more efficient. Birds can also control the blood flow by making the vessels wider or narrower. Their feet are kept just above freezing, cold enough to minimise heat loss but warm enough to stop any tissue damage. Incredibly, mallards lose only about 5 per cent of their body heat through their large feet in icy conditions – 95 per cent is lost from their much warmer heads and bodies.

Why do birds often stand on one leg? It's probably another adaptation to retain heat. By balancing on one foot, a bird halves the surface area exposed to cold water or ice and reduces heat loss even further. It also allows the lifted foot to dry out and warm up tucked in among the feathers. Flamingoes could potentially scupper this theory, because they live in warm water and often stand on one foot, except that they also have a heat exchange system for the opposite problem – to prevent them overheating. Another theory is that a bird is less likely to become stuck in the mud by periodically swapping from one foot to the other. Or it could just be more comfortable – just as we shift weight from one side to another when standing up for a long time.

A Royal Surprise

My husband, Rory, put his underpants on this morning and was stung by a wasp! Was it a queen? *Lisa*

What an unfortunate turn of events! Yes, any wasp seen at this time of year will be a queen, and those found in a house are likely to be from one of the eight species of social wasp in the UK. The rest of the colony – the female workers, male drones and old queen – all die off in the autumn and only young fertilised queens survive to hibernate through the winter. The queen finds a safe spot, tucks her wings and antennae out of the way and sits out the cold weather. She emerges in spring and starts building a walnut-sized nest in which she lays eggs that are fertilised with sperm stored over winter. Once the first batch of workers emerge they take over construction while the queen focuses on laying eggs. The wasps will then be kept busy catching insects to feed the growing larvae.

Queens that hibernate in our homes may wake up early due to the warmth of central heating and will starve if they can't find any nectar (although the larvae are carnivorous, the adult wasps often need nectar to survive). They will be quite dozy and may wander into piles of washing or wardrobes. The main purpose of a wasp's sting is to subdue prey so it can be transported back to the nest easily. Bees and wasps will also use the sting in defence when the nest is threatened or if a wasp finds itself in an uncompromising position – for example, stuck inside Rory's underpants!

The stings of bees and wasps are fascinating. The structure evolved from an ovipositor, a long tube used to lay eggs, which means that only female bees and wasps can sting. (The queen lays her eggs through an opening at the top of the stinger instead.) The stinger is usually hidden away inside the abdomen but is pushed out when a wasp or bee stings and acts like a hypodermic needle, injecting venom into the victim's skin. A barbed sheath surrounds the needle-like stinger and provides anchorage. A wasp's barbs are small so it can withdraw its sting, but the shaft of a honeybee's sting has larger barbs. These get stuck in thick, human skin, and when the bee tries to retreat, the end of its abdomen is ripped off, leading to death shortly afterwards. This may seem like a design flaw, but honeybees usually sting other insects, like hornets, that may be a threat to the hive, and because these have much thinner skin, the bee can withdraw and use its sting repeatedly.

Wasps don't leave their sting behind, but if you're unfortunate enough to be stung by a bee, the stinger should be removed as quickly as possible, as it can carry on injecting venom into the skin even after it has separated from the bee. Also, move away from the area to avoid further stings. Bees and wasps release pheromones when they sting, alerting other members of the colony to the potential danger and inciting them to join the attack.

As Rory probably discovered, a tiny amount of venom, perhaps a drop the size of a full stop, can inflict a huge amount of pain. Each species' venom is different, but they all contain a cocktail of proteins and enzymes that cause the reaction responsible for the intense stinging sensation. For people with an allergy, this reaction may escalate and could even trigger anaphylactic shock. If someone becomes breathless or develops a rash or swelling after being stung, they should seek medical help immediately.

Out of Place

I live in Twickenham, in southwest London. This morning we found a crab in the middle of our lawn. It was dark greenish grey in colour and about 5 centimetres in diameter. It was alive when we first found it but was dead an hour or so later. Do you have any idea how it could have got there? *Becca*

From the description and the location, this sounds like a Chinese mitten crab. As the name suggests, these crabs are far from home – they're native to East Asia but have been found in the Thames since 1935. They probably arrived in ballast water discarded from ships and are now found in several rivers across the country, including the Medway, Ouse, Tyne, Tamar and Dee. West London, including Twickenham, seems to be a particular hot spot. International shipping has spread these crabs across the globe, from Asia to Europe and North America.

Mitten crabs may look innocuous with their furry claws (the mittens), but these eight-legged invaders are making a nuisance of themselves in their adopted home. Unlike our indigenous shore crabs, Chinese mitten crabs spend most of their lives in fresh water. The crabs live in burrows dug into soft, muddy riverbanks and as the population grows they can cause the banks to collapse. Their digging can make the water muddy, which may silt up gravel beds that fish use for spawning. Mitten crabs may also have an impact on native species; they compete with other predators for food and could affect numbers of their prey such as invertebrates and fish eggs.

Once in a new place, the crabs spread easily – in China they have been known to migrate 1,500 kilometres up- and downstream to breed, so the journey from the Thames estuary to Twickenham is nothing to them. After four or five years, they head seawards and return to saltier water to breed. After mating, the females lay eggs that go through several larval stages before developing into juvenile crabs. These small crabs head upstream to start the freshwater phase of their life. Mitten crabs have been known to travel long distances overland on their way to and from the sea, even through gardens and streets, so the crab that Becca found could have been on migration. It could also have been dropped by a gull or other bird that had managed to catch it.

Mitten crabs have few natural predators in the UK and numbers in the Thames have increased at an alarming rate since the 1980s, possibly due to its cleaner water. There are now thought to be millions living in the capital but, potentially, there could be an ingenious solution to keeping their population in check. Mitten crabs are something of a delicacy in Asian cooking, especially the gonads, and so scientists have been testing crabs from the Thames to see if they are safe to eat and assessing how the culinary trade might play a role in controlling these alien invaders.

Weather Beaten

We noticed yesterday when it was snowing really hard that the birds were not coming to our bird feeder. There was no activity for a couple of hours. Do they have trouble flying in falling snow? Does the snow affect their judgement? *Foak*

Birds can fly through snow if they must but will choose to take shelter for a few hours if possible. Any motorist who has attempted to drive through a heavy snowstorm will appreciate that white-out conditions make navigating nearly impossible. While a driver can overcome this by crawling along at just a few kilometres an hour, birds need to fly at a certain speed to stay in the air so they will try to avoid flying in a blizzard. However, if it's cold enough to snow the birds will be under pressure to find food, so they may be forced to take to the wing.

Not all birds have the option of using bird feeders in bad weather, though:

> *We have three owls that live in a barn near our house and I was wondering why I have seen them out during the day, at midday and about 2pm in the afternoon. They are usually*

only around at dusk, so why they are out and about at that time of day? John

Individual barn owls differ enormously in their habits. Some are resolutely nocturnal while others are crepuscular – most active at dawn and dusk. Very few regularly hunt during the day but a period of adverse weather may occasionally force them to do so in daylight hours. The barn owl's hunting method relies on using their very sensitive hearing to locate prey, such as mice and voles. They have asymmetric ears, with one ear set higher on the head than the other, and this allows them to pinpoint the sounds of their prey scurrying through the undergrowth, even in pitch darkness. This hunting method does have its drawbacks, though. When it's windy, owls can't hear properly so they can't hunt effectively. Rain also poses problems, not just because of the sound issues but also because a barn owl's soft, fine feathers aren't very waterproof. Their plumage might be ideal for flying almost silently, but it's prone to waterlogging.

Fortunately, barn owls can usually afford to sit out a period of wet or windy weather. They can survive for a couple of days without hunting because they often have a cache of small mammals to see them through, especially during the breeding season. At other times of year, barn owls aren't terribly energetic birds and may roost for 22 hours a day, so they don't use many calories. Nevertheless, as soon as the weather clears up, hunger may encourage them to hunt in the daytime.

It's not just rain and wind that can cause problems for birds of prey:

How do owls and kestrels feed in fog? Liz

Fog may not be too troublesome for barn owls as long as they can still hear their prey, but it's a different story for kestrels because they depend on their excellent vision to find voles, mice and other small mammals. They hunt by scanning the ground from 10 or 20 metres above rough grassland, so thick fog seriously hampers their hunting.

Kestrels are known as 'windhovers' because they appear to hover effortlessly, even when buffeted about in high winds. By constantly making small adjustments to their wing and tail feathers, kestrels can keep their head and eyes steady and will spot the slightest movement from quite a distance. A kestrel can detect a beetle from 50 metres and dive on a small bird up to 300 metres away. Their acute eyesight is also sensitive to ultraviolet light so their vision has an extra dimension compared to ours. A kestrel's sharp eyes can pick out the urine trails left by voles and mice which glow in UV light and stand out against the vegetation. These act like a beacon guiding the kestrel to areas with most small mammal activity and revealing where it should focus its hunting efforts.

Kestrels need to eat several vole-sized meals a day and will often cache excess prey so they can raid the larder if bad weather persists. Starvation is the greatest threat to survival for kestrels, but fortunately fog rarely lasts long. Wind and rain are less of a problem – in wet weather kestrels can turn to worms and beetles to supplement their diet.

Petrol Heads

Noticing a strong smell of petrol in our garden today, I found that our nearly full 5-litre, plastic petrol can stored behind the shed was leaking badly and was nearly empty. The reason, incredibly, was several holes gnawed into the corners by what can only be a squirrel – the teeth marks are identical to those found on our bird feeders. What could have triggered this behaviour and has anybody else had a similar experience? *Graham*

Grey squirrels are the bane of many a gardener who is trying to feed the birds. There are squirrel deterrents that attempt to keep them away from bird feeders and some are more effective than others. Squirrels may be outwitted by baffles or 'squirrel-proof' feeders that are surrounded by a wire cage, especially if feeders are hung on thin rope or wire that the squirrels cannot clamber down. It's not easy to outfox a grey squirrel, though, because they can jump over or leap around many obstacles. Squirrels also have sharp teeth and powerful jaws that can crack nuts so they make short work of many plastic or wire defences.

It's easy to understand why squirrels attack birdfeeders but it's harder to discern why they would target a petrol can. It's doubtful that these grey squirrels wanted to drink the petrol in Graham's shed (or commit arson!). One clue is their front teeth; grey squirrels are rodents so their incisors grow continuously and to keep them in check they are prodigious chewers. In wild conditions they will gnaw on bark or bones to wear down and sharpen their teeth. Many foresters consider grey squirrels to be pests because they chew and strip bark from trees, sometimes causing extensive damage or even killing a tree. Our gardens provide many other things to nibble on such as hoses, and if they enter our homes they can chew through insulation, roof joists, telephone wires and water pipes. They will even bite through electrical cables, a habit that once proved fatal for a grey squirrel in Bill Oddie's shed. This can have very serious consequences for homeowners if the chewed wires cause a power cut or a fire. For this reason it's a good idea to try to prevent squirrels getting into your house or loft.

Squirrels have been known to chew through the fuel pipes and the brake cables of cars, although smaller rodents such as mice may be responsible for vandalising vehicles too. The rubber gas pipes attached to barbecues may also become a target. Why squirrels would choose to nibble on a petrol can or car parts is something of a mystery; there have been suggestions that the plastic tubing or outer coating contains certain substances like sodium that are lacking from the squirrel's diet. Squirrels have a good sense of smell so perhaps their interest would be piqued by the scent of petrol or brake fluid. Some people claim that squirrels are attracted by solvents or gas fumes and deliberately seek them out. It's not unknown for animals to become intoxicated on fermenting fruit so perhaps Graham's squirrels have turned to a new tipple?

Black-Beaked Blackbirds

I've been getting more and more blackbirds with black beaks in my garden and far fewer with the yellow/ orangey bill. What's going on? *Holly*

Blackbirds must be one of our most easily recognised garden birds. Adult male blackbirds are undoubtedly handsome, with their velvety black plumage and striking bright orange beak and eye ring. Females and juveniles are a little duller, with brown feathers and beaks. Why does the male have such a bright beak?

As always, it's down to sex. The colour of the male's beak is related to his weight, and females appear to prefer males with deeper orange beaks. Before blackbirds started inhabiting our gardens, they lived in dark forest canopies where the crocus-coloured beak would stand out in the gloom. Male blackbirds perform a courtship display, running with their heads bowed and beaks open, showing off the glorious orange bill and trying to impress the ladies. The blackbird's beautiful song has also been shaped by its woodland past – the notes need to be loud and powerful to penetrate the dense leaves and branches of the forest canopy.

The males only develop their distinctive yellow beaks and full black plumage once they're ready to breed in their second year. Until then, young males retain dark brown wings and a dark beak, so the males that Holly saw in her garden could be young birds in their first winter.

However, there could be another explanation, especially if the numbers of dark-beaked birds are rapidly increasing at this time of year. Many of our garden birds indulge in what's known as chain migration. This means that when large numbers of 'our' garden birds move south and west for the winter continental birds arrive to take their place. Ringing studies suggest that 12 per cent or more of the blackbirds we see in the UK in winter are visitors from Scandinavia and mainland Europe, coming to our shores to escape the hard weather and short days of their northern latitudes. Unlike British birds, these adult males have dark beaks during the winter months; their bills only turn yellow once they have returned to their breeding grounds in the spring. It's possible to distinguish young British birds with dark beaks from European migrants by taking a close look at their shape and colour. Scandinavian birds have longer wings so they appear sleek and slim next to the comparatively short-winged and plump residents. Immigrant blackbirds often have a slight grey tinge to the feathers, giving them an almost frosted appearance. Enjoy them while they're here!

Super-Cool Plants

My daughter wants to know why moisture in trees and plants doesn't freeze? *Lynne*

Sometimes the moisture in trees and plants does freeze and, as many gardeners know, icy conditions can kill plants. Plants are damaged when water inside their cells freezes and expands, rupturing the cell walls. The leaves blacken or turn brown and become limp, and often the affected part of the plant will die off. If the plant is tender or conditions are very bad the whole plant may be killed. So how do plants survive in sub-zero temperatures when covered by frost and snow?

There are two strategies: freeze avoidance and freeze tolerance. Annual plants can avoid freezing by overwintering as a seed but perennials must endure the winter. Some plants protect their tissues from freezing using a process called supercooling. The composition of moisture in their tissues is adjusted so that it can remain liquid well below the freezing point of water – it is supercool. Plants do this by removing water from the liquid in their cells and accumulating sugars or amino acids that make the solution too concentrated for ice to form at zero degrees. In the same way, the salt in seawater prevents it from freezing until it reaches about minus 2 degrees Celsius.

Another strategy is to tolerate ice formation in their tissues, but this only happens outside the cells where it causes less injury to the plant. The plants produce substances called ice nucleators that encourage water to crystallise outside the cells. Small ice crystals form in the gaps between cells and water is drawn out of the cell, making the solution inside more concentrated. This makes the fluid inside the cell less likely to freeze but runs the risk of damaging the cell through dehydration – most frost damage is caused by dehydration rather than the freezing itself.

Many plants also produce anti-freeze proteins. Despite their name, these proteins don't actually lower the freezing point but instead attach to ice crystals between the cells and slow their growth. They also prevent the crystals becoming too large and damaging the plant.

A plant's ability to tolerate cold weather fluctuates throughout the year. Overwintering plants need a period in which they can acclimatise to falling temperatures and become hardy. It takes time to produce the anti-freeze proteins and concentrate solutions within the cells. This process is triggered naturally in autumn as days become shorter and colder; however, a sudden unexpected cold snap out of season can damage plants that would normally be able to tolerate freezing conditions. Once spring growth starts, plants rapidly lose their hardiness.

Occasionally, cold weather can cause plants to produce frost flowers – spectacular ice crystals often seen on the trunks or stems. These occur when the plant's sap chills and expands, causing small cracks and tears in the plant's stem where the sap seeps out. The sap then freezes as it hits the cold air. If the ground isn't frozen, sap will continue to rise due to the capillary action in the plant's vessels, forcing out more sap. The crystals lengthen into ribbons, petals or fine 'hair' at right angles to the stem, creating natural ice sculptures called frost flowers or crystallofolia. These beautiful, delicate structures don't last long so it's worth keeping an eye out for them on morning winter walks.

Avian Obesity

Do birds get fat on fat balls? *Anthony*

The short answer is 'no'. Unlike humans, birds don't overeat – they can't afford to get too heavy because they need to fly. In fact, they have such high metabolisms that it would be difficult for them to ingest much more food than they need. Flying requires a lot of energy and birds burn many calories to keep warm, especially as they maintain their body temperature at a few degrees warmer than we do. In winter, small garden birds need to eat up to 30 per cent of their body weight in food every day just to survive the long, freezing nights. That's equivalent to an average 80-kilogram man eating a massive 25-kilogram sack of potatoes every day!

Birds flock into our gardens during cold weather, seeking out bird feeders. Over half of us feed the birds on a regular basis, providing an estimated 60,000 tonnes of bird food each year. Just think how many calories that food contains – it's a massive helping hand to small birds trying to survive, especially in snowy conditions.

It's best to provide a variety of food types for different birds. Fat is the most important ingredient at this time of year because it's so calorific. Fat balls are fantastic, though please remember to remove any plastic netting from shop-bought balls because birds' feet can become entangled in it. Protein is also important and can be found in mealworms or meat scraps. Peanuts (unsalted) and sunflower hearts are perfect because they're very calorie dense, packed with fats and oils. Birds will really appreciate a good-quality seed mix as well. Goldfinches particularly love niger seed, which is similar to their natural food of thistle seeds. Don't forget that water is vital too, for bathing and drinking, especially when birds are feeding on dry seeds. And don't stop feeding when the winter is over – birds appreciate extra food all year round, especially in spring when they are trying to raise a family.

Please don't feel obliged to offer gourmet meals, though – shop-bought bird food can be expensive and birds will happily finish off your leftovers or the contents of your store cupboard. Bits of stale cheese, unsalted bacon rind, cake, pastry, dried fruit, apples or other fruit, cooked (but not raw) rice, and suet will all be very welcome. Avoid butter or unsaturated fats, though, as these can clog up the birds' feathers. Of course, one of the easiest ways to serve bird food with the least effort is by planting shrubs and trees that will supply plenty of berries in the cold months. The fruits and berries of native species such as holly, ivy, rowan, hawthorn and elder provide a sugar hit, but exotic garden plants such as pyracantha, cotoneaster and berberis are just as good.

Feeding garden birds not only helps them make it through the toughest time of year, it also allows us to encounter wildlife without braving the elements – your generosity will be rewarded with fantastic close-up views. If you keep an eye on your feeders you can help out with vital research too. The British Trust for Ornithology collects weekly data from householders about which birds they see for their Garden Birdwatch survey. If that seems too onerous, the RSPB run an annual Big Garden Birdwatch at the beginning of each year that takes only an hour to complete. Both organisations would be glad of your information on sightings to provide an insight into how garden birds are faring across the year and in the long term.

Winter Wardrobe

I was wondering what are the cues used by animals that change the colour of their fur or plumage in winter? Is it something like day length or temperature, or a combination of factors? I'd imagine it could be pretty disastrous if they get it wrong, as they would stick out like a sore thumb, so would be more likely to be predated or to be spotted while hunting. Also, if climate change does mean we will see less snow, will this disadvantage animals who do change their coat colour? *Dan*

The only animals that regularly change colour in winter in the UK are ptarmigan, stoat and mountain hare, with the occasional report of a white weasel. In summer they are various shades of brown but in autumn they moult and grow new white fur and feathers. Ptarmigan and mountain hare are both upland species, living on exposed moorlands and mountains with few hiding places. Camouflage is vital to avoid predation so they have evolved to merge into the background in every season. In spring and summer they're difficult to see against the green and brown vegetation, but snow is common in winter so they turn white.

Stoats are more widespread across the country and not all develop a white ermine coat in winter; populations in the south of the UK often stay brown all year. This is partly due to genetics – studies have shown that if southern stoats are transported to the north they can't turn white in winter, and vice versa. As Dan suggests, a stoat of the 'wrong' colour would stand out like a sore thumb and would soon be spotted by its prey or caught by a predator, such as a golden eagle. Presumably, centuries of selection pressure from predators have shaped each population, making the genes for turning white more prevalent in northern populations and practically redundant in the south.

Moulting into a new coat is triggered by the photoperiod – the day length. The animal's eyes take in information about the amount of light available per day and that is communicated to the hormonal system which in turn produces a compound called melatonin. When melatonin levels rise, the production of pigment decreases, so when the animals grow new feathers or fur they are white. Although the moulting process is prompted by day length at a certain time of year, the speed of this change is controlled by air temperature. At altitude, where it's cold, a stoat can change in a matter of a few days while lowland stoats may take up to a month. This makes sense because it allows the animal to be flexible and respond to local weather conditions. It would be crazy to turn completely white in the middle of a balmy October or November but it would be a huge advantage to change coats quickly during a cold snap.

In autumn, the stoat's moult starts with its feet and belly and progresses up the flanks and head. In spring the moult is reversed, starting at the nose and working down the body. This means the belly and legs keep the thicker fur for longest because they are the parts most likely to get cold.

If climate change leads to winters with consistently less snow, the mountain hare and ptarmigan could suffer. They are living at their limits on the hills and can't shift to a higher altitude or move further north.

Waste Management

On Saturday we discovered a dead fox in our back garden, lying under a tree. Dead wild animals are not often seen – or are they? Where do they go? *Bill*

Few wild animals have the luxury of a comfortable old age. As soon as they become weak or ill, most will be targeted by a predator so their body would soon disappear. Large mammals, such as foxes, have fewer enemies, but if they are in poor condition they will quickly succumb to starvation or disease. It's common for sick or injured animals to seek shelter and hide out of harm's way. If they die, we are unlikely to come across them. Foxes will often take refuge under a shed or in their underground earth (burrow) so it's unusual to find one out in the open. Perhaps it experienced a sudden death from a fight or fast-acting poison.

Wherever they fall, dead animals don't go to waste – far from it. Thankfully, there's a whole community of species that rely on carrion or the country would soon be knee-deep in corpses. When an animal dies, it provides bed and board for others. Scavengers like crows, ravens, red kites, rodents, foxes and many birds of prey will break open a large carcass and eat much of the flesh. This makes the remains more accessible for smaller species.

Many flies, including bluebottles and other blowflies, quickly detect a fresh carcass and are among the first visitors. They lay hundreds of eggs that soon hatch into hungry maggots. These grow rapidly by consuming the dead tissue before crawling off to pupate into adult flies, which in turn provide food for birds, frogs and toads.

Millions of bacteria and fungi are also essential for the body to decay completely. Some of these originate from within the animal while others are found in soil or air. Bacteria multiply and grow, breaking down proteins, carbohydrate and fats in the remains. The carcass becomes putrid, changing colour and giving off the distinctive smell of death that is repellent to our noses but irresistible to many insects and scavengers.

As the body decomposes, new species arrive to take advantage of this valuable resource. Wasps, ants, slugs and all sorts of invertebrates will take a bite of flesh. Various types of beetle colonise carcasses – some eat the dead animal while others feed on the fly eggs and maggots. Sexton beetles, also known as burying beetles, are nature's undertakers; they specialise in burying the bodies of small mammals and birds. Their antennae pick up the sulphurous chemicals given off as the corpse decays and they hurry to the body where a turf war may ensue. A pair of sexton beetles will fight off others to take ownership of the body before digging around the dead animal and burying it. The female lays her eggs in the buried body, which provides food and shelter for the growing larvae. Sexton beetles are attentive parents and, unlike most insects, both sexes take care of the brood. They protect the larvae until they pupate and become adults.

The speed of the carcass' decomposition depends on a number of factors, including temperature and the availability of oxygen. In rare circumstances, if the remains are buried quickly they may be preserved or even become fossils over the course of many millennia. Usually, though, with the help of all these different decomposers, most bodies will be broken down within a few days or weeks until just the skeleton and fur or feathers remain. Even the bones will be gnawed by animals trying to retrieve the calcium.

It may not be a glamorous lifestyle, but these creatures and microbes that live on the dead perform a vital job. There are finite supplies of minerals and elements such as nitrogen in each ecosystem and they need to be recycled. These unsung heroes make nutrients available to other species and convert dead tissue into living plants and animals. It's a simple fact of life that birth and growth cannot happen without death and decomposition.

Colour Blind

I have noticed recently that all or most water or sea birds, especially the ones which feed from the surface of the water, are predominantly white, e.g. gulls, eider ducks, smew, terns, egrets and herons, swans, great crested grebes, plovers, etc. I assume it's because the white plumage is better 'camouflage' on the water surface? *Gingernut*

There are several different types of camouflage that help animals to merge into their surroundings. Many animals, not just birds, are darker on top than underneath and have a pattern of colouration called countershading. Sunlight illuminates an object from above, so if it is all one colour the object appears lighter on the upper side and darker in the shade underneath. Artists exploit this pattern of light and shade to make an object jump off the page and appear three-dimensional. For most animals that want to avoid being eaten or need to sneak up on prey, the last thing they want to do is 'jump off the page'. They want to be inconspicuous. By having a dark colour above and a lighter shade below they offset the shadows cast by natural light and make themselves less visible.

Countershading is common across many different kinds of animals but it is particularly prominent in marine species such as sharks, dolphins, penguins and fish. If viewed from above, these animals are camouflaged against the dark deep sea, and if seen from below, it's difficult to distinguish them from the bright sky. In many species, the dark colours on the upper side gradually merge into the light colours on the belly, so if the animal is seen from the side the camouflage is still effective.

Birds like herons that rely on stealth to fish from above the water's surface also benefit from countershading. Many sea ducks such as smew, eider ducks and long-tailed ducks use another kind of camouflage. The males of these ducks have beautiful black and white plumage that appears quite striking on land but breaks up their outline when bobbing about on the sea. It's known as dazzle camouflage and it doesn't necessarily conceal a bird but confuses any predator trying to judge its shape and location. A similar strategy was adopted by naval ships during the First World War. An ornithologist called John Graham Kerr advised Winston Churchill to paint battleships with geometric patterns similar to zebra stripes. Before the days of radar and other sophisticated detection systems boats had to be spotted by the human eye. In theory, the dazzle camouflage would create optical illusions, breaking up the boat's outline and making it harder for the enemy to determine the boat's distance and direction. The museum ship HMS *Belfast* is painted in dazzle camouflage and the practice continued throughout the Second World War. Recently, this camouflage had a bit of a revival and a few American navy ships are decorated with geometric patterns. Although this wouldn't be effective against modern radar, it may still confuse anyone taking aim at the vessel.

In a Tight Squeeze

My daughter wishes to know if there are any known cases of badgers with claustrophobia. *Steve*

What a brilliant question! Clearly, it would be a massive disadvantage to any animal that lives in an underground burrow or sett to have a fear of confined spaces. Fortunately, it's unlikely that a wild animal would develop a phobia like that. Phobias are defined as irrational fears and are usually caused by an unpleasant experience or trauma, often in childhood. People with claustrophobia may be scared of getting stuck in lifts, tunnels, small rooms or any other confined space. The fear can be so great that it triggers a panic attack. People and animals aren't born with phobias but develop them over time; in other words, it's a learned response rather than an innate behaviour. In humans, phobias can be treated with therapy and controlled exposure to whatever causes the fear.

Animals often display fear, though, and it's a useful survival tool. Many are instinctively afraid of apparent threats, such as snake-shaped objects, and will be startled by loud noises. This innate wariness increases the animal's chance of avoiding injury or death. Animals also learn to fear certain things that hurt them – once bitten, twice shy – though this could hardly be described as an irrational fear as it's a rational response to danger.

Pets can develop phobias if they learn to associate a particular object or experience with pain or distress. For example, a cat may resist going into a carry box if it was used to take it to the vet, or a dog may hate the vacuum cleaner even if it has never caused him any harm. Badgers are sometimes caught as part of biological studies, and like most animals they certainly dislike being confined in a trap, which is completely understandable and so doesn't really constitute a phobia. In fact, badgers are probably most comfortable and cosy underground. The idea of living in a dark sett may be objectionable to us, but for a badger its home is a place of safety and warmth.

Winter Quiz

1. Which of your garden birds is a true featherweight? Put these in order, heaviest first:

   A. Blackbird
   B. Goldcrest
   C. Great tit
   D. Wren

2. If an ornithologist studies birds and an entomologist studies insects, what do these people study?

   A. Dendrologist
   B. Lepidopterist
   C. Bryologist
   D. Paleontologist

3. Which fictional action hero was named after an American ornithologist?

   A. Luke Skywalker
   B. Indiana Jones
   C. James Bond
   D. Clark Kent (Superman)

4. Which species of tree, often found in churchyards, is believed to live up to 2,000 years or more?

    A. Oak
    B. Beech
    C. Sweet chestnut
    D. Yew

5. What kind of creature is a lumpsucker?

    A. Grasshopper
    B. Fish
    C. Beetle
    D. Worm

6. If a rabbit lives in a warren, which animals live in these homes?

    A. Holt
    B. Sett
    C. Earth
    D. Drey

Winter Quiz Answers

Question 1 Answer:

A. Blackbird (100 grams) based on the weight of an average adult

C. Great tit (18 grams)

D. Wren (10 grams)

B. Goldcrest (6 grams)

Question 2 Answer:

A. Trees

B. Butterflies and moths

C. Mosses and liverworts

D. Fossils and prehistoric life

Question 3 Answer:

C. James Bond. The real James Bond was an expert on Caribbean birds and wrote the definitive book on the subject, *Birds of the West Indies*. The author Ian Fleming was a keen birdwatcher living in Jamaica and chose the ornithologist's name for his hero apparently because it sounded 'as ordinary as possible'.

Question 4 Answer:
D. Yew trees. Many are older than the churches they shadow, and are thought to mark previous pagan places of worship or burial grounds.

Question 5 Answer:
B. It's a fish, often found in rockpools at low tide. The lumpsucker has specially adapted fins forming a suction disc on its belly, allowing it to 'stick' to rocks and resist being washed away by the waves.

Question 6 Answer:
A. Otter
B. Badger
C. Fox
D. Squirrel (red or grey)

Sources of Information and Inspiration

If you want to know more about a particular plant or animal, or you've been inspired to get involved, here's a list of UK wildlife and conservation organisations that would love to hear from you. Many of these organisations have local branches and all rely on the help of volunteers – so get outside and have fun!

ARC Trust – the Amphibian and Reptile Conservation Trust's activities include managing 80 nature reserves, working with schools, researching and monitoring species' populations in the wild and campaigning for the protection of amphibians and reptiles.

> **Web:** www.arc-trust.org
> **Address:** 655A Christchurch Road, Boscombe,
>   Bournemouth, Dorset BH1 4AP
> **Tel:** 01202 391319
> **E-mail:** enquiries@arc-trust.org

Bat Conservation Trust - devoted to the conservation of bats and the landscapes on which they rely. BCT supports dozens of local bat groups, monitors bat populations and seeks to inspire people about these under-appreciated mammals.

Web: www.bats.org.uk
Address: 5th floor, Quadrant House, 250 Kennington Lane,
London SE11 5RD
Tel: Bat Helpline 0845 1300 228
E-mail: enquiries@bats.org.uk

British Dragonfly Society - working to conserve dragonflies and their wetland habitats. The BDS promotes the study, recording and appreciation of these exquisite flying jewels and their aquatic larvae.

Web: www.british-dragonflies.org.uk
Address: c/o Natural England, Parkside Court, Hall Park
Way, Telford TF3 4LR
Tel: 0300 060 2338/07792 231 925
E-mail: questions@british-dragonflies.org.uk

British Hedgehog Preservation Society – funds research, runs surveys and gives advice to the public on the care of hedgehogs, particularly when injured, ill or in any other danger.

Web: www.britishhedgehogs.org.uk
Address: Hedgehog House, Dhustone, Ludlow, Shropshire SY8 3PL
Tel: 01584 890801
E-mail: info@britishhedgehogs.org.uk

British Trust for Ornithology (BTO) – an independent charitable research institute that organises many citizen science surveys and welcomes data from volunteers.

Web: www.bto.org
Address: The Nunnery, Thetford, Norfolk IP24 2PU
Tel: 01842 750050
E-mail: info@bto.org

Buglife: The Invertebrate Conservation Trust – dedicated to the less glamorous, often overlooked species of insects, spiders and earthworms. There are over 40,000 invertebrate species in the UK and Buglife is dedicated to 'conserving the small things that run the world' with plenty of surveys you can help with.

Web: www.buglife.org.uk
Address: Bug House, Ham Lane, Orton Waterville,
    Peterborough PE2 5UU
Tel: 01733 201210
E-mail: info@buglife.org.uk

Butterfly Conservation – saving butterflies, moths and their wider habitats. Owing to their sensitivity to environmental change, moths and butterflies are good indicators of the health of the countryside and you can help gather valuable data. BC also takes care of over 30 nature reserves.

Web: www.butterfly-conservation.org
Address: Manor Yard, East Lulworth, Wareham, Dorset
    BH20 5QP
Tel: 01929 400209
E-mail: info@butterfly-conservation.org

The Conservation Volunteers – formerly known as the British Trust for Conservation Volunteers, TCV has local groups across the UK that run practical conservation days and 'Green Gyms' to encourage you to get fit while helping wildlife!

Web: www.tcv.org.uk
Address: Sedum House, Mallard Way, Doncaster DN4 8DB
Tel: 01302 388883
E-mail: information@tcv.org.uk

Froglife – national wildlife charity dedicated to the conservation of the UK's amphibians and reptiles (frogs, toads, newts, snakes and lizards) and the habitats on which they depend.

Web: www.froglife.org
Address: 2A, Flag Business Exchange, Vicarage Farm Road, Peterborough PE1 5TX
Tel: 01733 558844
E-mail: info@froglife.org

Hawk and Owl Trust – conserving owls and other birds of prey in the wild by creating and managing habitats for them, carrying out practical research and increasing public appreciation of them (many birds of prey are still persecuted).

Web: www.hawkandowl.org.uk
Address: PO Box 400, Bishops Lydeard, Taunton TA4 3WH
Tel: 0844 984 2824
E-mail: enquiries@hawkandowl.org.uk

The Mammal Society – organisation dedicated to the study and conservation of mammals in the British Isles. They support a large network of mammal experts and enthusiasts, and you can help to survey and monitor mammals, learn more about them and secure their future.

Web: www.mammal.org.uk
Address: 3 The Carronades, New Rd, Southampton
  SO14 0AA
Tel: 023 8023 7874
E-mail: info@themammalsociety.org

Marine Conservation Society – working to protect our seas, shores and wildlife, the MCS campaigns for marine protected areas and sustainable fishing. You can join in with beach cleans and, if you're a diver, take part in underwater surveys.

Web: www.mcsuk.org
Address: Unit 3, Wolf Business Park, Alton Road, Ross-on-Wye, Herefordshire HR9 5NB
Tel: 01989 566017
E-mail: info@mcsuk.org

National Trust – as well as serving over 3.5 million cups of tea every year and protecting historic houses and gardens, the National Trust is the UK's biggest landowner and looks after large areas of coastline and countryside. You can join the thousands of volunteers who help to manage their land or try one of their conservation holidays (though you have to pay for these).

Web: www.nationaltrust.org.uk
Address: PO Box 574, Manvers, Rotherham S63 3FH
Tel: 0844 800 1895
Email: enquiries@nationaltrust.org.uk

People's Trust for Endangered Species – varied conservation work including projects on dormice, stag beetles, traditional orchards and general mammal surveys that you can take part in.

Web: www.ptes.org
Address: 15 Cloisters House, 8 Battersea Park Road, London SW8 4BG
Tel: 020 7498 4533
Email: enquiries@ptes.org

Plantlife – working to protect our wild plants and fungi. Plantlife campaigns against invasive non-native plants and manages over 20 nature reserves. You can participate in their national Wildflower Count survey or help with conservation work days in the field.

Web: www.plantlife.org.uk
Address: 14 Rollestone Street, Salisbury, Wiltshire SP1 1DX
Tel: 01722 342730
E-mail: enquiries@plantlife.org.uk

Pond Conservation – half of the UK's ponds were lost in the twentieth century and 80 per cent of those that remain are in a poor state so Pond Conservation are encouraging people to create ponds and protect freshwater wildlife. They'd also like the results of any pond dipping and records of frog- and toadspawn.

Web: www.pondconservation.org.uk
Address: c/o Faculty of Health & Life Sciences, Oxford Brookes University, Gipsy Lane, Headington, Oxford OX3 0BP
Tel: 01865 483249
E-mail: info@pondconservation.org.uk

Royal Society for the Protection of Birds (RSPB) – originally set up in 1889 to campaign against the trade and use of feathers in women's hats, the RSPB now has over a million members and aims to conserve all biodiversity, especially wild birds and their habitats. They also coordinate the Big Garden Birdwatch at the beginning of each year, an easy activity for all the family that has produced important scientific data over the past 30 years.

Web: www.rspb.org.uk
Address: The Lodge, Sandy, Bedford SG19 2DL
Tel: 01767 680551

Shark Trust – advocates for management and protection of these much-maligned creatures in the UK and abroad. The Trust would love any records of shark, skate and ray purses (also known as mermaid's purses) or any sightings of sharks.

Web: www.sharktrust.org
Address: 4 Creykes Court, 5 Craigie Drive, The Millfields, Plymouth, Devon PL1 3JB
Tel: 01752 672020
E-mail: enquiries@sharktrust.org

The Vincent Wildlife Trust – carries out research and surveys to assess how well our mammals are faring. They have a particular interest in pine martens, pole cats, stoats, dormice and bats. They also manage over 40 reserves, primarily for bats.

Web: www.vwt.org.uk
Address: 3 & 4 Bronsil Courtyard, Eastnor, Ledbury, Herefordshire HR8 1EP
Tel: 01531 636441
E-mail: enquiries@vwt.org.uk

Whale and Dolphin Conservation (WDC) - established back in 1987, WDC is dedicated to the conservation and welfare of whales and dolphins, also known as cetaceans. Over 25 species inhabit UK waters and WDC funds research, education and campaigns on marine issues.

Web: www.whales.org
Address: Brookfield House, 38 St Paul Street, Chippenham,
   Wiltshire SN15 1LJ
Tel: 01249 449500
E-mail: info@whales.org

Wildfowl and Wetlands Trust (WWT) - founded in 1946 by Sir Peter Scott, the WWT focuses on wetland conservation. It has over 200,000 members and nine wetland reserves across the UK.

Web: www.wwt.org.uk
Address: WWT Slimbridge Wetland Centre, Slimbridge,
   Gloucestershire GL2 7BT
Tel: 01453 891900
E-mail: enquiries@wwt.org.uk

The Wildlife Trusts – there are 47 local wildlife trusts across the UK, with over 800,000 members and a network of 2,000 nature reserves. They're a great way to get involved with wildlife in your patch and have a thriving youth section called Wildlife Watch. To find your local trust go to:

Web: www.wildlifetrusts.org
Address: The Kiln, Waterside, Mather Road, Newark, Nottinghamshire NG24 1WT
Tel: 01636 677711
E-mail: enquiry@wildlifetrusts.org

The Woodland Trust – works to protect our woods and encourages people to plant native trees. The trust has planted over 16 million trees and runs a number of projects to inspire people including Nature's Calendar, a survey of the changing signs of spring and autumn that you can help by submitting your records of seasonal events.

Web: www.woodlandtrust.org.uk
Address: Kempton Way, Grantham NG31 6LL
Tel: 01476 581111
E-mail: enquiries@woodlandtrust.org.uk

Acknowledgements

The biggest thanks must go to the fabulous *Springwatch* audience for sending in such perplexing and interesting questions and to the *Unsprung* host and guru, Martin Hughes-Games, for inspiring and nurturing such unique programmes. Huge thanks to all our *Springwatch* conservation partners but especially Paul Stancliffe and Graham Appleton at the BTO for sharing their immense knowledge so readily; to the *Springwatch* production team for their support, especially Tim Scoones and Ailish Heneberry who championed the proposal for this book and Holly Spearing for encouragement; to Julia Koppitz and Myles Archibald at HarperCollins for their guidance and patience; and finally thanks to my supportive friends and family who listened to my woes and eased the writer's block.

About the Authors

Joanne Stevens has worked in natural history TV and radio for 13 years. She is one of the producers of *Springwatch*, *Autumnwatch* and *Winterwatch*, more recently appearing on-screen as 'Level-headed Joe' in the *Unsprung* series. She gained a first-class BSc degree in Zoology and an MSc in Conservation Biology. More importantly, she loves enthusing about the natural world and has a lifelong passion for British wildlife. She'd rather be outside. Unless it's raining.

Martin Hughes-Games has worked in television for over 30 years. He was a producer on *Springwatch* and *Autumnwatch* before going over to the 'other side' and becoming part of the presenting team. Martin was host of the very first *Unsprung* when he arrived by motorbike – and he has been there ever since. He used to race motorbikes and is a keen climber and chicken fancier.

Index

adder 62
  baby 71–2
  eggs 60, 62
  venom 71–2
aerial plankton 66, 80–2
Africa 6, 33, 42, 43, 62, 66, 82,
    168, 169, 170, 197, 201
amplexus 44
ants:
  black garden 85
  carcasses and 237
  flying 85–6
  nests 37
apophallation 70
aposematism 110
apteria 76
ARC Trust 249
Arctic 150, 169, 197
Arctic terns 60, 62
Autumn 127–87

baculum 123, 125
badger 7
  claustrophobia 241–2
  diet 118, 119–20
  hedgehog and 88
  inherited setts 118–19, 245,
    247

rabbits as prey 54
raiding fox larders 115
traditional name 184, 186
urban 118–20
watching 7
winter activity 154, 189–90
barn owl 35
  bad weather and 222–3, 224
  eggs 35
  hunting 97–8, 223
  individuals differ in habits
    223
  nestboxes and 200
  use roads to navigate
    96–8
Barn Owl Trust, The 97
Bass Rock 68
Bat Conservation Trust 250
bats:
  hanging upside-down, adverse
    effects of 48–9
  birth 77
  carrying babies 77–8
  greater horseshoe 77
  hibernation 154, 155, 190
  horseshoe 78
  moths and 105
  phobia of 185, 187

beaver's tail 214–15
bees:
　attitudes towards 95
　bumblebees 8–9, 108, 203–5
　cold/wet weather and 107–9,
　　203–5
　helping in the garden 9
　hibernation 8, 203–5
　honeybees 19, 108, 203–4,
　　219
　phobia of 185, 187
　sleep-like status 19
　sting 218, 219
　'warm up' flight muscles 8–9
　what can you do if you find
　　soggy? 108–9
beetles:
　carcasses and 69, 237–8
　glow-worms 125
　kestrel and 224, 225
　ladybirds see ladybirds
　sexton 69, 237–8
　stag 70, 256
Bempton 68
Big Garden Birdwatch 233, 257
birds:
　aerial insect/plankton and
　　80–2
　angry 15–16
　beaks 133–5
　bird box 199–201
　brood patches 76
　circulatory lungs 152
　cultural learning 52–4
　dimorphic 46–7
　fat balls and 231–3

feeding upside-down 180–1
first flight 78–80
fledglings 13–15
foreplay 60–2
heaviest garden bird 244
hoarding of food 137–9
how can a tiny bird lay three or
　four eggs that have a total
　volume similar to that of
　themselves? 34–5
imprinting 41–3
loudest call 152–4
male and female difference
　46–8
migration 60, 62, 66–7,
　148–9, 168–70, 178, 192
　see also under individual bird
　name
nesting in precarious positions
　78–80, 93–4
number of feathers on 75–6
predominance of white colour
　in water or sea 239–40
scent and nest 28–9
snow's effect upon 222–5
song, learning 172–3
which birds lay most eggs in
　one go? 34–5
bittern:
　call 152–3
　population restoration
　　153–4
black-backed gull 91
blackberries 127, 148, 174
blackbird 46
　colour of beak 227–8

how do they detect worms or invertebrates in the soil? 88-90
night, activity at 202-3
song 172-3, 201, 202-3
squirrels and 161
blackcap 169-70, 202
blue tit:
  angry 15-16
  breeding season 15, 211-12
  chest of male 46
  cultural learning 53-4
  feathers 75
  fledgling 13-15
  nest, scent and 28-9
  nestboxes and 211-12
Bond, James 244, 246
brambles 127
British Dragonfly Society 250
British Hedgehog Preservation Society 251
British Trust for Ornithology (BTO) 75, 97, 98, 212, 233, 251
'Brocco Bank' 118
brood patches 76
buff-tailed bumblebee 204
bumblebee 8-9, 108, 203-5
butterflies 9
  brimstone 129
  cold weather and 174-5
  fritillary 56
  grizzled skipper 124
  helping in the garden 9
  hibernation 129
  migration 81, 174-5

  red admiral 174-5
  spider webs and 144
  UK species 107
Butterfly Conservation 252
buzzard 54, 156, 207-8

caecotrophic 215
camouflage 27, 71, 85, 94, 135, 152, 234-5, 239-40
caterpillar:
  ecdysis 57
  great tit and 35, 149
  growth 57
  tent-making 56-8
cats:
  communication 32-4
  domestication 32-3
  glottis 33
  purring 32, 33-4
caudal autonomy 142
Cetti's warbler 152
chicken: egg-laying 5, 36-7, 114-15
Churchill, Winston 240
chutney 127-8
chimpanzees 16, 51, 125
clinting 131
coal tit 137-8
coat colour change 234-6
Conversation Volunteers, The 253
corncrake 201
Cornwall 135, 141, 207
countershading 239-40
cowbird, brown-headed 43
crab: Chinese mitten 220-2

crested tit 137
crows:
    attack foxes and birds of prey
        156–8
    hooded 138
    play 195–7
crystal brain fungus 163
cuckoo: imprinting 41–3
cultural learning 52–4
curlew 93, 113, 134

daffodil, wild 61, 63
Darwin, Charles 46, 211
dawn chorus 8, 202
dazzle camouflage 240
death:
    seeking shelter and 236
    where do animals go after
        236–8
deer:
    red 131
    rut 131, 162, 163
    shed antlers 131
deer mice 40–1
dimorphic 46
dog vomit slime mould 163
dogs:
    attraction to fox poo 26–7
    sense of smell 26–7
    yawning 51
dolphin 68
    bow-ride 116–18
dormouse, hibernation of 154,
        190
dream: do oysters/shellfish? 18,
        20

duck:
    beaks 133, 134
    cold legs when standing in
        cold water 216
    countershading 239, 240
    dazzle camouflage and 240
    eider 240
    eye-catching male 46
    filial imprinting 42
    foxes steal eggs of 115
    long-tailed 240
    nests 76
Dunkery Beacon 162
dunnock:
    cuckoo and 42, 43
    foreplay/sexuality 20–2

earthworm 119, 202, 207, 209,
        210, 211
ecdysis 57
eggs:
    foxes stealing 115
    how can a tiny bird lay three or
        four eggs that have a total
        volume similar to that of
        themselves? 34–5
    which birds lay most eggs in
        one go? 34–5
    would two chicks grow/hatch
        from a fertilised double-yolk
        egg 36–7
    see also under individual species
        name
eider duck 239, 240
Eimer, Theodore 103
elderflower blossom 65

ermine moth 56, 57–8

Fair Isle 68
female choice, concept of 46
filial imprinting 41–3
fledglings 13–15
flycatching 111
foreplay, bird 20–2
foumart 122, 124
fox 189
    calls 197, 198
    crows and magpies attack 156
    cubs 24–6
    mating 198
    play 198
    poo, dogs attraction to 26–7
    red 197
    scent 27
    shelter during death 236
    stealing eggs 115
    vixen helpers 25, 26
    winter activity 197–8
fritillary butterfly 56
'frog jelly' 164
frogs:
    far from water 84–5
    frogspawn 162, 164
    tadpoles and 73–4
    vulnerability to birds 142
FSC (Field Studies Council) 69

geese 34–5
    Arctic and 169
    bar-headed 151
    barnacle 150
    brent 150, 169

egg-laying 34–5, 42
graylag 150
height of flight 150, 151–2
honking during flight 150,
    151
migration 150–1, 169
nests 76
pink-footed 150
V-shape flying 150–1
white-fronted 150
Gerald of Wales 6
Germany 100, 103, 110, 169,
    170
glow-worm 123, 125
goldcrest 169, 244, 246
goldfinch 61
Grandry corpuscles 134
grass snake 60, 62
great tit:
    brood timing 35, 149
    cultural learning 53–4
    egg-laying 35
    food storage 137
    mobbing 157
    nestboxes and 212
    song 173
    weight of 244, 246
Greenland 150
grey partridge 35
grey wagtail 15
grouse 46, 93
guffing 7
gull:
    black-backed 91
    Dartmoor and 91, 92–3
    herring 91, 92

inland 91–3
   mobbing 80, 157
   nesting 78–9

hare 7–8
   mountain 234, 236
Hawk and Owl Trust 254
hedgehog:
   'hedgehog street' 190–1
   hibernating 154–6, 190, 204
   lifespan 184, 186
   spines 87–8
   raiding foxes larder 115
hen harrier 93
Herbst corpuscles 134
heron:
   brown 152
   chicks 31
   countershading 240
   diet 30–1
   do they get cold legs when
      they stand still in cold
      water? 216–17
   garden ponds and 31
   hunting 30, 31
   'nick' moorhen chicks 31
   'standing still' 30
   'walking slowly' 30
herring gull 91, 92
hippocampus 138
hobbies 168
homing instinct 39–41
honeybee 19, 108, 203–4, 219
hornets 129, 219
horsehoe bat 77, 78
house martin 80, 81

house mice 39–41
humpback whale 68

Iceland 150, 178
Invertebrate Conservation Trust,
   The 252
Ireland 68
Irish Sea 68
Isla 7
ivy 129, 174, 200, 232

jay:
   colours of 129–30
   hoarding 138–9

Kerr, John Graham 240
kestrel:
   feathers, number of 75
   feeding in bad weather 224–5
killer whale 68
kin selection 25
King, Simon 7–8, 68
kittiwake 78, 91
knot: beak 134–5
koi carp, toad mating with 44–5

lackey moth 56
ladybird:
   communication 146–7
   name 110
   reflex blood 110
   sacred reputation 110
   seven-spot 147
   species of 109–10, 123
   spots of 2, 109–10
lapwing 93

Lent lily (wild daffodil) 61, 63
limpet:
  clinging onto rock 17
  do they return to the same
    place each time the tide goes
    out? 17–18
  grazing 18
  'mushroom' 17–18
  radula 18
  toughness of 17
linnet 172–3
lizard:
  caudal autonomy 142
  common 62
  egg-laying 60, 62
logger, building a 70
long-tailed duck 240
long-tailed tit 24
lumpsucker 245, 247

magpie 16
  harass foxes 156, 157
  intelligence 16
  mirror test and 16
  nest 90, 91
  sparrowhawks prey on 100,
    101
mallard 23, 46, 114–15, 217
Mammal Society, The 254
Marine Conservation Society
  255
marsh tit 137
martin 82, 168
  house 80, 81
  migration 168
Massie, A. M. 69

meadow pipit 42
mealworm 172, 232
melatonin 235
'mermaid's purse' 122, 124
milk thieves, birds as 53–4
mobbing 157–8
mole:
  above ground 102
  breathing underground 102
  Eimer's organs 103
  eyes/eyesight 102–3
  high blood oxygen affinity
    104
  how do moles meet? 102–4
  hunting 90, 209
  mating 103–4
  name 184, 186
  skin 103
  smell 103
  tunnels 104
moorhen:
  chicks, herons 'nick' 31
  nidifugous 23
  parenting 23–4
moth 9
  attraction to light/artificial
    light 105
  burnet 105
  cinnabar 105
  compound eyes 105
  ermine 56, 57–8
  finding way in dark 105–6
  lackey 56
  migrations 66–7
  'neural summation' 105–6
  nocturnal 105

nocturnal flight 82, 83
'Silver Y' 67
speed of flight 67
trap 66, 107
'twitchers' 66
variety of 107
moulting 88, 136, 140, 179, 234, 235
mouse:
deer mice 40–1
doormouse 154, 190
harvest 77
house 39–41
navigation 39–41
mute swan 178–9, 184 186

National Trust 255
Natural History Museum 69
Nature's Calendar 148
newt 7, 84
great-crested 184, 186
nightingale 201
nightjar 72, 201
Norfolk 12, 135, 153
nostoc 163
Nottingham Trent University 78
nuthatch 180–2

On the Origin of Species (Darwin) 46
OPAL initiative 69
Orkney 68
Osprey 60, 62
oystercatcher 184, 186
oysters: do they sleep and dream? 2, 18–20

Packham, Chris 7, 129
pandiculation 50
peacock 46, 175
penguin 76, 165, 239
penis bone 125
People's Trust for Endangered Species 256
peregrine falcon 70, 190
maiden flight of 78–80
Petworth Park, West Sussex 131
Phenology 148, 149
phobias 185, 187, 241
pigeons:
crop milk 164–5
deformed feet of feral 213–14
feeding chicks 164–5
homing 96
mating in October 164–5
sparrowhawk preys on 101
using roads to navigate 96–8
pipistrelles 78
plant moisture, freezing of 229–31
play, function of 195–7
Pliny the Elder 112
poikilothermic (cold-blooded) animals 73–4
poison pie 185, 187
polecat 54, 122, 124
polyandry 21
polygynandry 21
polygyny 21
pond, digging a 192
Pond Conservation 257
ptarmigan 234, 236

pterylae 76
puffin 98–9

quiz:
  autumn 184–7
  spring 60–3
  summer 122–5
  winter 244–7

rabbit:
  badgers and 119
  breeding 54, 55
  caecotrophic 215
  hierarchy 55
  predators/mortality rates 54, 55
  red kite and 207
  why do they have white, furry bottoms? 54–6
ramsons (wild garlic) 5
  early rising 166–7
raptor 185, 187
raven 63, 196, 236
red admiral 174–5
red kite:
  conservation of 205–6
  diet 207, 236
reed warbler 42, 43
reflections, birds attacking 15–16
reptiles, egg-laying 60, 62
rescue centre, local 9, 156
Richmond Park 131
robin 15
  bird box and 199, 200
  egg-laying 34, 35

friendly nature 170–2
huddling together 12
late night song 201–3
lifespans 184, 186
mating 47–8
sexual differences in 46–8
rock pooling 67
roundworm 27
Royal Society for the Protection of Birds (RSPB) 257

salmon 130–1
salt licks 159–60
Savernake Forest, Wiltshire 205
Scandinavia 150, 169, 228
Scilly Isles 135
Scotland 33, 68, 135, 148, 181, 206
Scottish Wildcat 33
sea cliffs 68
seabirds 35, 68, 99, 216–17 *see also under individual species name*
seal 68
  why are baby grey seals born white? 135–6
sex ratio 21
sexton beetle 69, 237–8
sexual imprinting 42, 43
sexuality 20–2
Shark Trust 258
shark 122, 124, 239
Shetland 68
Siberian tit 138
Skomer Island, Wales 68, 98
skylark 93, 94, 172–3

sleep:
    brainwave patterns during 19
    dreams and *see* dreams
    relaxed muscles during 19
    REM 20, 83
    shoreline creatures and
        18–20
    slow-wave (SWS) 83
slime moulds 163
slowworm:
    egg-laying 60, 62
    hatching 141–2
    hibernation 142
    mating 142
    name 141
slugs 70
    small or orchard 57
smew 239, 240
snail:
    common garden 11
    common pond 12
    do they get slower with age? 2,
        11–12
    edible or Roman 11
    feeding 67
    'foot' 67
    garden 60, 62
    hibernation 11
    how long to they live? 11–12
    movement of 12
    radula 67
    species 11
    weather and 11
snipe 133, 134
'snorkel trail' 67
Snowdonia 162

sources of information and
    inspiration 249
sparrow:
    bird box and 199–200
    cultural learning and 52–4
    eating your house 158–61
    grit and feeding 158–9
    hedge 20
    house 29, 52, 53, 158–61,
        199–200
    lifespan of 52–4
    tree 52
sparrowhawk:
    drowning prey 100–1
    hunting 100–1, 189, 190
spider 81
    biggest house spider in UK 128
    cardinal 128
    house spider ('daddy longlegs')
        128
    invade houses during autumn
        139–41
    large webs between trees
        143–4
    mating 140
    medical applications of web
        145
    strength of webs 144–5
    Tegenaria house spider 139
    use of wind to move around 81
    what do they do with old
        webs? 144
spring 5–64
squirrel:
    burial of nuts 176–7
    calcium and 160–1

courting 190
diet 160–1
feeders and 225, 226
grey 161, 176–7, 225, 226
nest/dreys of 90–1
petrol and 225, 226–7
red 161, 176, 225
salt licks 159–60
teeth/chewing 225–7
stag beetle 70
star jelly 162–3
starling:
  bird box and 199–200
  cultural learning and 53
  migration 192
  mimics 112–14
  murmerations 192–3
  nest, scent and 28–9
  sparrowhawks hunt 100–1
stoat 54, 234–5
Summer 65–126
swallow 5
  migration 6, 60, 62, 148, 168
  nesting 65
swan 34–5
  Bewick's 178, 179
  cygnets 179
  migration 178
  mute 178, 179, 184, 186
  protection for 178–80
  Queen and 178
  Swan Upping 179
  whooper 151, 168–9, 178,
    179
swift:
  catching insects 80, 81, 82

lifespan 82
mating 65
migration 60, 62, 82, 168
nesting 65
screams 61, 63, 66, 82
sleeping on the wing 19, 65,
  66, 82, 83
two years of ceaseless flight
  65, 82

tadpoles 45, 73–4, 84, 164
tapeworm 27
tern, Arctic 60, 62
thigmotaxis 39–40
tits *see under individual tit name*
toad:
  mating 44–5
  migrating 6–7

Vincent Wildlife Trust, The 258
vulpine 61, 63

waders 42, 93, 134, 216–17
wagtail:
  grey 15
  hunting 111
  pied 111
  why do they wag their tails?
    111–12
wallfish 60, 62
warbler:
  Cetti's 152
  nests 93–4
  reed 42, 43
wasp:
  hornets *see* hornet

queen 218–21
reputation 95–6
sting 218–21
wood and 94–6
waterfowl:
  beaks 134
  chicks 23, 35, 42
  cold 76
  see also under individual species name
waxwing 169
weasel 54, 190, 234
web cameras 70
Whale and Dolphin
  Conservation (WDC) 259
whale:
  humpback 68
  killer 68
  watching 68
wildcats: do they purr? 32–4
Wildfowl and Wetlands Trust
  (WWT) 179, 259
wildfowl 216, 217 *see also under
  individual species name*
Wildlife and Countryside Act,
  1981 179
Wildlife Trusts, The 260
willow tit 137
windows, birds attacking
  reflections in 15–16
winter 189–247
woodcock 94, 169
Woodland Trust, The 148, 260
woodlice 184, 186
woodpecker:
  great spotted woodpecker 38

green woodpecker 37–8, 184,
  187
lesser spotted woodpecker
  38
tails 181
why doesn't it break its beak
  when it hammers on a tree?
  37–9
woodsmoke 127
World Snail Racing
  Championships, 1995 12
worms:
  blackbirds detect in the soil
    88–90
  during floods, do they drown?
    208–11
  earthworms 119, 202, 207,
    209, 210, 211
  glow-worms *see* glow-worms
  mating 209–10
  mealworms 172, 232
  migration 209
  moles and 103
  roundworms 27
  tapeworms 27
  slowworms 62, 141–2
wren:
  bird box and 199
  call 152, 202
  roosts en masse 212
  weight 244, 246

yawning: animals and 50–1
yew trees 245, 247

zugunruhe 169

Accompanies the BBC TWO TV series

Join the *Springwatch* team as they guide you through Britain's rich and diverse natural world, and enjoy the nation's wildlife at its finest.

Springwatch: British Wildlife is the perfect introduction to the much-loved wildlife of the popular television series – how they live and where to find them, why they do what they do and how we can learn to appreciate them.

You will be introduced to the birds, mammals and plants that inhabit our gardens, cities and countryside, with detailed species descriptions and beautiful photographs allowing you to understand their appearance, behaviour and habitats.

Discover the best-kept secrets about garden birds, fascinating fungi facts and what leaves and seeds tell us about our thriving plant life. Join the *Springwatch* team as they help you to explore the natural world and unlock the mysteries of British wildlife.

Available in hardback
ISBN 978-0-00-746286-5
UK £20